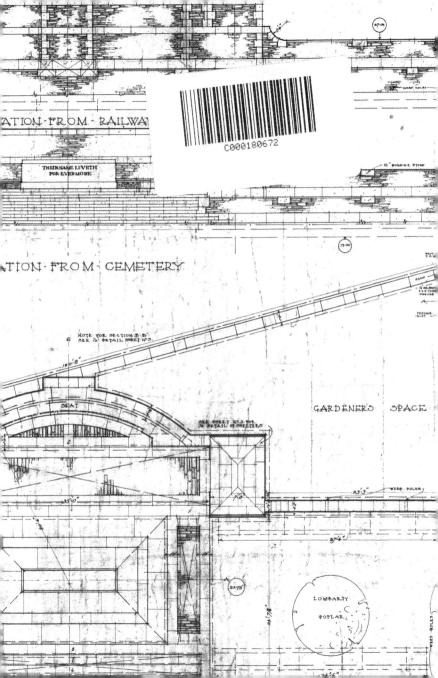

...ATION·FROM·RAILWA...

THEIR NAME LIVETH
FOR EVERMORE

C000180672

...TION·FROM·CEMETERY.

GARDENER'S SPACE

SEAT

LOMBARDY
POPLAR

Epitaphs of the Great War: The Last 100 Days

For Nigel

EPITAPHS OF THE GREAT WAR:
THE LAST 100 DAYS

SARAH WEARNE

UNIFORM

1918
2018

UNIFORM

Uniform
an imprint of Unicorn Publishing Group

Unicorn Publishing Group
5 Newburgh Street
London W1F 7RG
www.unicornpublishing.org

First published by Uniform 2018
© Sarah Wearne 2018, © Unicorn Publishing Group, 2018

A CIP catalogue record for this book is available
from the British Library

ISBN 978-1-911604-62-4

Printed and bound in Czech Republic

Photograph on page 14–15:
Commonwealth War Graves Commission
All other photographs kindly provided by Andrew Holmes

ACKNOWLEDGEMENTS

I should like to thank the Commonwealth War Graves Commission for their help with this book, in particular Victoria Wallace for agreeing to write the foreword, and Max Dutton for his help with my research. I am very grateful to Andrew Holmes who has allowed me to use some of his beautiful photographs of the war cemeteries, which add so much to the atmosphere of the book. Neither this nor my other two books of epitaphs could have existed without the technical support of my son, Harry Wearne, who set up and manages my Twitter account @WWInscriptions and its associated blog, epitaphsofthegreatwar.com. But then the books themselves would never have come about without Ryan Gearing of Uniform, who followed me on Twitter, suggested that I wrote the books and then, with his team, made such an excellent job of their production. And lastly I must thank my husband, Nigel, who has never complained at the number of holidays we have spent perusing the battlefield cemeteries, nor at the number of hours these books and the Twitter project have consumed over the past four years.

Do you remember that hour of din before the attack, –
And the anger, the blind compassion that seized and shook you then
As you peered at the doomed and haggard faces of your men?
Do you remember the stretcher-cases lurching back
With dying eyes and lolling heads, – those ashen grey
Masks of the lads who were once keen and kind and gay?
Have you forgotten yet? ...
Look up, and swear by the green of the Spring that you'll never forget.

Aftermath
Siegfried Sassoon 1919

Only the dead have seen the end of war

Soliloquies in England and Later Soliloquies
George Santayana 1922

FOREWORD

The building of the war cemeteries around the world following the First World War was likened by Kipling to a work the scale of which had previously only been undertaken by the pharaohs. The Imperial War Graves Commission got it so right in the equality of treatment, and the simplicity and dignity of design, leading to the erection of some of the most iconic memorials in the world. So it is almost impossible to believe that they then got it so wrong – by charging the bereaved next of kin by the letter for their inscriptions – a policy which outraged some member Governments and which was later dropped.

I will always wonder whether the shortest – "RIP", "Beloved" and just "Jim" were the result of grief beyond words, or that of poverty. But it did have one positive effect. We perhaps forget that a world used to paying by the letter for telegrams was rather good at articulating important, often life-changing messages into very short phrases. The law of unintended consequences perhaps, and the result of this enforced economy were even more powerful in concentrating the mind.

When I learned of Sarah's project to collect and publish these epigrams and tell their stories I was absolutely delighted. These short lines are some of the Commission's real treasures; on display around the world, yet too often overlooked. I have never mastered the art of the quick cemetery inspection, being invariably waylaid by the headstone inscriptions. The words offer not only an insight into the sentiments of the families, but of the world in which they lived; one in which religious texts, Shakespeare and poetry, learned by rote, were embedded in popular culture in a way in which perhaps the lyrics of rock anthems or strap lines from classic movies are today. They nevertheless have the power to move modern audiences; almost every day, I see the inscriptions photographed and quoted on social media. The few short words reach through the decades and should we ever forget, remind us of the man.

As I travel around the world visiting just some of our 23,000 sites I am regularly floored by the simplicity of the articulation of love, grief, pride, loss and occasionally anger that is carved in stone for perpetuity. Sometimes the inscriptions offer an insight into the men and women who died – a reference to their career, their sporting prowess, or to their family. Others show the painful reconciliation the family had made with their god and their nation, and with the war which had caused their loss. Even today, when we rebury soldiers recovered from the fields of France and Belgium, families are invited to choose an inscription. In March 2018, when we finally laid to rest Durham Light Infantryman, Private Thomas Edmundson, their chosen epitaph – so appropriate after 103 years was "I once was lost, but now am found."

The 1400 staff of the Commonwealth War Graves Commission today work to ensure that our cemeteries and the resting places of all 1.7 million servicemen and women remain accessible and well cared for. Our mission is eternal, and the six member Governments continue to fund us in proportion to the losses they suffered. Far from retreating from this obligation with the passage of time, when the Commission marked its centenary, the members adopted a new strategy recognising that their role now had grown, being both guardians of the graves, but also for new generations, custodians of the memory. We want to help visitors to our sites to see the stories behind each headstone.

Each one of these epitaphs, these tiny testimonials to lost love, is as significant to the CWGC as any one of its magnificent memorials to the missing. We are honoured to be the perpetual guardians of these final goodbyes.

Victoria Wallace
Director General
Commonwealth War Graves Commission

TYNE COT CEMETERY

PREFACE

On 8 August 1918 the Allied armies launched a surprise attack along the Western Front. By the end of the day they had advanced eight miles, created a fifteen-mile gap in the German lines, taken 12,000 prisoners and over 300 guns. Although no one then knew it, this was the beginning of the end, the opening of what is now known as The Last 100 Days, which finished on 11 November 1918 with the Allied victory. To the historian Gary Sheffield this 'forgotten victory' was 'by far the greatest military victory in British history'. However, today's public, still possessed by the disasters of the Somme and Passchendaele, scarcely notice it. Yet meticulous staff work, successful deception, efficient logistical support, good intelligence, accurate gunnery and the development of integrated 'all-arms' attacks had transformed the British Army. It was no longer the one that had struggled through the early years of the war, it was now a highly effective fighting force, which contributed in no small way to the victory.

This is the third book in a series. The first two looked at one hundred personal inscriptions from the graves of men and women who died during the Somme and Passchendaele campaigns; this book covers the dead of the last 100 days. There are in fact only ninety-six days between the 8 August and 11 November inclusive, nevertheless, this is how the last campaign of the war is known and I have kept to this.

The huge cemeteries of the Somme and Passchendaele demonstrate the static nature of those campaigns. The frontline cemeteries of these final months move steadily eastwards. Some of them only holding the dead of a couple of days before the battle moved on. But as with all the war dead, it could be several years before the Imperial War Graves Commission asked the next-of-kin to check the accuracy of the information that would be carved on the headstone and suggest a personal inscription. One 1918 casualty's inscription even refers to the number of years that have passed: 'We who loved him only know how much we lost eight years ago'. This means that what families chose to say was not an instant response to the death of their loved one but something influenced by the passage of time.

Each book is a product of my Twitter project, @WWInscriptions, which has Tweeted a personal inscription every day since 4 August 2014 and will do so until 11 November 2018. The idea was inspired by the fact that both Twitter and the Commission restricted the number of characters people could use – although the Commission's sixty-six character limit was less than half that originally allowed by Twitter. This letter restriction means that many of these inscriptions are masterpieces of compact emotion – especially as each letter cost 3½ old pence so there was no desire to waste them. But their enforced brevity can sometimes hinder our comprehension, and the passage of time has definitely obscured their meaning for us. When families quoted from the Bible, hymns, the Book of Common Prayer, referenced historical events or literary passages, they confidently expected their contemporaries to recognise the context. Being less familiar with these sources today we don't necessarily pick up the references or understand the allusions: 'In loving memory these are they – ' refers to a hymn where the 'they' are those who went from great suffering to dwell with Christ; 'He tried to do his duty' is what a nineteenth-century Imperial hero, Sir Henry Lawrence, killed at the Siege of Lucknow, asked to have put on his grave; 'He played the man', Latimer's words to Ridley as they prepared to be burnt at the stake, is a reference to martyrdom by means of a terrible death for a noble cause. In order to make each inscription more comprehensible, each Tweet is attached to a blog post at epitaphsofthegreatwar.com, which provides context both for the inscription and for the casualty. The research has thrown up stories of underage soldiers, false identities, family scandals and family tragedies that continue into the Second World War.

The Commission initially intended inscriptions to be in the nature of a religious text or prayer. In addition they gave themselves the right to censor those they thought unsuitable. After all, they reasoned, it was 'clearly undesirable to allow free scope to the effusions of the mortuary mason, the sentimental versifier, or the crank'. However *The Times* disagreed, arguing:

> The heart of the bereaved may be in an epitaph which may seem absurd to people in another class of life; nor, by the way, is it at all certain that later generations will confirm the judgement of contemporary culture.

Posterity does indeed judge differently and it's the informal, 'human' inscriptions that speak most poignantly to us today: 'The shell that stilled his true brave heart broke mine' garnering infinitely more 'likes' and retweets than the patriotic, 'True to the flag'.

The inscriptions have all been selected for the insight they provide into the way people at the time thought, highlighting for example a huge variety of responses to the war: 'What cruel folly is war it robs us of our dearest'; 'His last message "I would not have missed it for anything"', 'He counted his very life as not too much to give for England'. They indicate the numerous causes for which people believed they had been fighting: 'He gave his all for freedom the whole wide world to save'; 'He fought and died for his wife and little son and to save his country'; 'For the glory of England and the honour of Bristol';

'For Canada and the Empire'; 'He fought for Scotland and for South Africa'; 'He gave up all he loved to fight for the freedom of the world'. Inscriptions also reveal the central role played by duty: 'He volunteered / he thought it was his duty / he died that we might live'; 'He left for the front in sadness o'ercast but duty was duty with him to the last'; 'His last words "I am not afraid I have done my duty"'; 'He detested the whole atmosphere of war but did his duty'.

Inscriptions reveal the strength of people's faith, their acceptance of God's will, 'Thy will be done' being one of the most popular of all inscriptions, or 'We cannot Lord Thy purpose see but all is well that's done by thee', and even, 'Not my will O Lord but thine be done'. Belief in the afterlife was strong too, from the relatively secular, 'Until we meet again' and 'Not lost but gone before' to 'He is not here he is risen'. And despite the Church's disapproval, there is also evidence of Spiritualism, the belief that the dead can communicate with the living through the offices of a medium: 'Yet he is here with us today a thousand things his touch reveal'; 'Though absent in body thank God he still talks with us'.

Inscriptions individualise the casualties: 'He was our only child'; 'Bright, intelligent lad was respected & loved by his regiment'. They throw light on the make up of the British army with its Welsh – 'Tros ryddid a'I wlad' (For freedom and country) – and its Scottish soldiers – 'Gus am bris an la agud an teach na sgaillean' (Until the day breaks and the shadows flee away). And on the make up of the British Empire with its Finnish Canadians –'Lepaa rauhassa rakastettu ja kaivattu' (Rest in peace beloved deeply missed) and Danish Australians – 'Kaere son vi modes snart', (Dear son we will meet again soon). Inscriptions indicate the social mix of the army: 'Dearly beloved son of Mr and Mrs Smith Post Office, Keose, Stornoway'; 'Youngest son of the Duke and Duchess de Stacpoole, Co. Galway, R.I.P.' They record the Americans who joined the British army before the United States entered the war: 'A volunteer from the USA to avenge the Lusitania murder'; 'An American citizen'. They reveal the political controversy over conscription in Australia: 'Better a wooden cross than be one who could have gone and did not', and over Home Rule in Ireland: 'Religion Church of Ireland an Irishman loyal to death to King and Country'; '"An Irish volunteer" he died for the freedom of small nations'.

Grief is the predominant theme: 'Oh God why did you take my all my heart has a wound that will never heal'; 'You were all the world to me Jimmy'; 'This grave holds all that life held dear'. Another strong theme promises that the dead will never be forgotten: 'Your mother does not cease to think of you for a single moment'; 'You are never forgotten Jack dear for true love never dies'.

There were families who criticized war: 'The purposes of life misunderstood'; 'An only son "to what purpose is this waste?" *S Matt. 26.8*'; 'If this is victory then let God stop all wars, his loving mother'. And those who questioned what it had all been about: 'He gave his sweet young life what for?'; 'Did he die in vain?' There were the straight talking relations: 'All this sad old world needs is just the art of being kind, Doll'; 'Would that those who made the quarrels were the only ones to fight', and those who left impenetrably enigmatic messages: 'Yes Dad'; 'Because'; 'Same message'.

The three books all examine what *The Times* called, 'the heart of the bereaved', the thousands of silent voices that speak from the war cemeteries, voices that stand at the opposite end of the commemorative spectrum to the Cenotaph; the one an austere, silent tribute to the Empire's dead, the other a clamour of voices: each one a tribute to an individual whether the 'Fourth son of the Earl of Albemarle' or 'Our dear old Sid'. These inscriptions, regularly dismissed in the past as no more than sentimental platitudes, have been hiding in plain sight at the foot of the Commission's headstones for nearly a hundred years. In 1912 GK Chesterton wrote of the people of England 'that have never spoken yet'. After 1918 thousands of bereaved people 'spoke' but perhaps no one has listened to them before. What you will discover is that they don't speak with a single voice.

Sarah Wearne
Bampton
June 2018

Cemetery construction underway at Daours Communal Cemetery Extension, France. October 1922. Courtesy of CWGC

AND THY NEIGHBOUR
AS THYSELF

PRIVATE ANDREW NOEL YOUNG
CANADIAN INFANTRY
DIED 8 AUGUST 1918 AGED 23
BURIED CAIX BRITISH CEMETERY, FRANCE

When Jesus was asked, 'Which is the first commandment of all?' he answered:

> Thou shalt love the Lord thy God with all thy heart, and with all thy soul, and
> with all thy strength, and with all thy mind; and thy neighbour as thyself.
> St Luke 10:27

According to *St Mark 12:30-1,* 'there is none other commandment greater than these', and
to *St Matthew 22:40,* 'on these two commandments hang all the law and the prophets'.
This being the case, the 1914–18 war was a spectacular example of mankind disregarding
God's law, something Mrs Lucy Young was keen to highlight in the inscription she chose
for her son. His inscription is a reprimand to all the belligerents.

Andrew Noel Young was born in Glasgow on the 10 December 1897. He attested
in Victoria, Canada, on 1 November 1917 giving his address as a hotel in Los Angeles,
his name as Andrew Macdonald, and that of his father as James Macdonald – neither of
which was true. Young's father was called Andrew Young and in 1917 he and his wife
lived in New Jersey, USA. But despite the fact that the United States had entered the war
on the side of the Allies seven months earlier, Young preferred to enlist in the Canadian
rather than the US army – nascent loyalty for the land of his birth, or perhaps to escape
parental disapproval?

Young served with the 7th Battalion Canadian Infantry and was killed on the opening
day of the Battle of Amiens when the battalion crossed the River Luce and took the
village of Cayeux, 'with very slight loss having met with no organised enemy resistance
during the advance' [Battalion War Diary.] Young was one of the two soldiers from the
battalion killed that day.

"IF ONLY"
FROM MUM

PRIVATE RICHARD BURR
LONDON REGIMENT (ROYAL FUSILIERS)
DIED 8 AUGUST 1918 AGED 19
BURIED IN BEACON CEMETERY, SAILLY-LAURETTE, FRANCE

This is not simply a wistful cry – although it could well be – but the title of a sonnet by Christina Rossetti (1830–1894) lamenting a time that has gone:

> If I might only love my God and die!
> But now he bids me love Him and live on,
> Now when the bloom of all my life is gone,
> The pleasant half of life has quite gone by.
> My tree of hope is lopped that spread so high,
> And I forget how summer glowed and shone,

Mrs Emily Burr chose the inscription for her son, Richard, the third of her six children. John, his older brother, had been killed three years earlier at Loos on 27 September 1915 whilst serving in the 1st Battalion Scots Guards. He has no grave and is commemorated on the Loos Memorial.

Born in October 1898, Richard Burr was called up in October 1916 and sent to France in October 1917. He served with the 4th Battalion London Regiment (Royal Fusiliers) and was killed in the trenches on 8 August 1918.

> Battalion War Diary 4th–8th August
> Bn in front line trenches. The period passed unusually quietly, there being very little artillery activity by the enemy. Our patrols were very active during the hours of darkness. Defences were strengthened and trenches improved.

A JOLLIE GOOD BOOKE
WHEREON TO LOOKE
WAS BETTER TO ME THAN GOLD

CORPORAL HUGH MILROY GILCHRIST
CANADIAN INFANTRY
DIED 8 AUGUST 1918 AGED 25
BURIED CAIX BRITISH CEMETERY, FRANCE

Corporal Gilchrist's father, Thomas Gilchrist, chose his inscription from a poem of uncertain authorship and date, his choice indicating his own original turn of mind and, by the change in tense between the inscription and the last line of the verse, his son's love of reading.

> O for a booke and a shadie nooke, eyther in-a-doore or out;
> With the grene leaves whisp'ring overhede, or the streete cryes all about.
> Where I maie reade all at my ease, both of the Newe and Olde;
> For a jollie goode book whereon to looke is better to me than golde.

Born in Edinburgh in 1892, Gilchrist and his family emigrated to Canada in 1911. They lived in Toronto where Gilchrist worked as a draughtsman. He attested in April 1916 and served with the 4th Battalion Canadian Machine Gun Corps. On the 8 August 1918 the machine gunners were allocated to various assaulting infantry battalions on the opening day of the Battle of Amiens. Gilchrist was killed near Fresnoy where the enemy machine gun fire was said to have been intense.

STATE NOT "HE NOBLY LIVED OR OTHERWISE; FAILED OR SUCCEEDED" FRIEND JUST SAY "HE TRIED"

CAPTAIN CHARLES POOLEY MC
DRAGOON GUARDS (PRINCESS CHARLOTTE OF WALES'S)
DIED 9 AUGUST 1918 AGED 45
BURIED CAIX BRITISH CEMETERY, FRANCE

A To a Soldier
Say not of him 'he left this vale of tears',
Who loved the good plain English phrase
'He died',
Nor state 'He nobly lived (or otherwise)
Failed or succeeded' – friend, just say
'He tried'.
O.E. (Somewhere in France.)

Published in the *Eton Chronicle* on 11 May 1916, the above verse had a very limited circulation so it is not obvious how Captain Pooley's widow came across it. Charles Pooley was not an Old Etonian.

Pooley joined the army as a private in 1890 and served continuously with the 5th Dragoon Guards until his death in France in August 1918. A Regimental Serjeant Major on the outbreak of war, he went with the Expeditionary Force to France on 15 August 1914. Just over a month later he was commissioned 'for valour in the field'. In January 1915 he became one of the first recipients of the Military Cross and by February 1918 he was an acting staff captain at brigade headquarters.

On 8 August 1918 the Brigade took part in the opening day of the Battle of Amiens. The war diary gives an almost hour by hour sometimes minute by minute account of events between the 8th and the 10th, reporting that at 2.55 pm on the 9th:

> The valley from Caix to the station was being heavily shelled by 5.9s. One of these landed in the midst of Bde. H.Q. killing Capt. Pooley MC (Staff Capt.) Lieut. H. Fry (Signalling Officer), Lieut. G. Hulbert 18th Hrs (Galloper to the G.O.C.) and two O.R.s and wounding Major Walter (O.C. 2nd M.G.S.) and Lieut. Frere 2nd M.G.S. besides causing about 10 casualties to the horses.

"CURST GREED OF GOLD WHAT CRIMES THY TYRANT POWER HAS CAUSED" VIRGIL

PRIVATE VICTOR LIONEL SUMMERS
CANADIAN INFANTRY
DIED 9 AUGUST 1918 AGED 31
BURIED ROSIÈRES COMMUNAL CEMETERY EXTENSION, FRANCE

Perhaps a better translation of this aphorism would use the word 'manifest', meaning is evidence of, rather than 'cause' since what Virgil was saying was that many crimes are evidence of the greed for gold. The sentiment is similar to the biblical words in *Timothy 6:10:* 'For the love of money is the root of all evil'.

Victor Summers's cousin, W de V Summers of Berkeley, California, chose his inscription, sounding as though he was one of the many people who held the view that the war was the result of imperialist tensions caused by world capitalism; a view still held by the Socialist Party of Great Britain:

> What was responsible for these wars was the whole world system of capitalism with its competitive struggle for profits and its collection of competing armed states.
> *Socialist Standard* September 2009

Summers was born in Clapham, Surrey in 1887 and educated at Ardingly College. He attested in Watrous, Saskatchewan on 28 October 1916 and served with the 28th Battalion Canadian Infantry. On 9 August, the battalion formed part of the attack on the village of Rosières, which is where Summers was killed. A year later, his body was exhumed from its temporary grave and buried in the military cemetery there.

SHOT DOWN AT DAWN
OVER THE GERMAN LINES
FAITHFUL UNTIL DEATH

LIEUTENANT RICHARD STONE
ROYAL AIR FORCE
DIED 9 AUGUST 1918 AGED 19
BURIED HEATH CEMETERY, HARBONNIÈRES, FRANCE

The words are 'shot down at dawn' not 'shot at dawn; Richard Stone was a pilot with 203 Squadron who at midnight on 8 August 1918 was attached to 201 Squadron in a ground attack role. The next day he took off in Sopwith Camel D6250 in support of the British troops attacking near Rosières. Driven off once by German fighters he returned to the area where he was attacked again. This time his plane was hit and crashed. Stone was killed.

As was the custom with pilots, the cut down propeller of his plane formed the cross over his original grave. It now hangs in the church of St Nicholas, Piddington, Oxfordshire. There is another survival from this crash. In May 1919, Stone's body was exhumed by the Australian Graves Detachment and reburied in Heath Cemetery. One of the Australians removed Stone's signet ring and when he was passing through London he returned it to Stone's father, John Morris Stone, a Lincoln's Inn barrister. The ring is still worn by a member of the Stone family.

The last line of Stone's inscription comes from the *Book of Revelation 2:10*. This quotes Jesus's promise, 'Be thou faithful unto death, and I will give thee a crown of life': a special reward for those who have met death in their efforts to fulfil God's will. As far as Stone's family were concerned, God's will was that they should defeat the Germans.

HE SHALL MASTER AND SURPRISE
THE STEED OF DEATH
FOR HE IS STRONG

PRIVATE JOHN PERCIVAL OSMOND MM
ROYAL BERKSHIRE REGIMENT
DIED 11 AUGUST 1918 AGED 19
BURIED AIRE COMMUNAL CEMETERY, FRANCE

During her lifetime the poet Elizabeth Barrett Browning was more popular than her husband Robert Browning, but this is not reflected in war grave inscriptions. Robert Browning comes close to Tennyson in the number of times he is quoted, but not so his wife.

This inscription comes from her poem *A Drama of Exile*. It recounts the events of Adam and Eve's first day in exile from the Garden of Eden, and their conversations with Gabriel, Lucifer, various angels, spirits, phantasms, and Christ in a vision.

On the Day of Judgement, when the trumpet shall sound and the dead shall be raised up, who will control Death, the pale horse of *Revelation 6: 7-8*? The second semichorus promise that:

> Yet a Tamer shall be found!
>
> ...
>
> He shall master and surprise
> The steed of Death.
> For He is strong ...

The Tamer will be Christ, he will overcome death for, 'as in Adam all die, even so in Christ shall all be made alive' *I Corinthians 15:22*. This is the meaning of Osmond's inscription: there is no death.

John Percival Osmond was born and brought up in South Molton, Devon where his father was a domestic groom and coachman. He served in the 2nd/4th Battalion Royal Berkshire Regiment and had been at the front for three months when he died of wounds received in action that day. The battalion had been part of an attempt to establish a bridgehead across the Plate Becque. But everything had depended on silencing the German machine guns and this did not happen. The attack failed.

MY TASK ACCOMPLISHED
AND THE LONG DAY DONE

PRIVATE ROY DOUGLAS HARVEY
ROYAL SCOTS (LOTHIAN REGIMENT)
DIED 11 AUGUST 1918 AGED 26
BURIED BOUCHOIR NEW BRITISH CEMETERY, FRANCE

Roy Harvey's inscription comes from W.E. Henley's poem *Margaritae Sorori*:

> ... The sun,
> Closing his benediction,
> Sinks, and the darkening air
> Thrills with a sense of the triumphing night –
> Night with her train of stars
> And her great gift of sleep.
>
> So be my passing!
> My task accomplished and the long day done,
> My wages taken, and in my heart
> Some late lark singing,
> Let me be gathered to the quiet west,
> The sundown splendid and serene,
> Death.

Harvey was a pupil at Hillhead High School, Glasgow, his war service covered in their war memorial volume. According to this: Harvey was struck by a bullet and killed 'instantaneously' following a gallant and successful attack. This wasn't how the battalion's war diary saw it. They certainly took part in an attack but it failed:

> ... for the following reasons, (a) the tanks were half an hour late and
> were all put out of action before crossing our front line (b) barrage line
> 400 yds too far advanced and missed German front M.G. positions (c)
> wire almost impenetrable.

Described as a reserved, thoughtful boy, noted for his thoroughness, accuracy and precision, it was totally in keeping that a Collins Gem dictionary, and a diary written up to the day before his death, should have been found on his body.

A WHITE MAN
AND TRUE FRIEND
SADLY MISSED

SAPPER VINCENT O'SULLIVAN
AUSTRALIAN TUNNELLING CORPS
DIED 11 AUGUST 1918 AGED 40
BURIED HERSIN COMMUNAL CEMETERY EXTENSION, FRANCE

Vincent O'Sullivan had no family, the only information the War Graves Commission had on him was that he was 'native of Ireland'. His inscription was written by Mr S.J. Millane, Brown Hill, Kalgoorlie, Western Australia, who also filled in O'Sullivan's circular for the Roll of Honour of Australia. Here, in the section that asks for the form-fillers relationship to the soldier, he has written 'friend and partner'. He meant business partner. They were prospectors. Otherwise, all Millane knew about his friend was that he was 'about 40 years' and that he had served in the Boer War having enlisted in Ireland.

Millane has composed a really touching tribute for his friend, describing him as 'a white man', not meaning a man with a white skin but a man who was good company, decent and trustworthy – a good bloke.

Vincent O'Sullivan enlisted on 24 March 1916, giving his occupation as 'miner'. He served, as many miners did, in the Australian Tunnelling Corps, laying cables, digging saps, trenches, dug-outs and mines. On 11 August 1918, the war diary of the 3rd Australian Tunnelling Company reported that O'Sullivan was one of five men who died 'owing to hostile aircraft bombs dropped on billet at Bracquemont'.

DIED TO SAVE AN ENEMY

PRIVATE SAMUEL BREW
AUSTRALIAN ARMY MEDICAL CORPS
DIED 16 AUGUST 1918 AGED 42
BURIED DAOURS COMMUNAL CEMETERY EXTENSION, FRANCE

Samuel Brew's brother, Captain Henry Brew, chose his inscription, confirming this statement when he filled in the circular for the Roll of Honour of Australia by saying: 'Killed while succoring [sic] wounded enemy'.

Brew served in the 6th Field Ambulance, their war diary records the circumstances of his death:

> 15th August: ... At about 12 noon the driver of a Ford Car stationed at Quarry X.4.s.8.3. (No. 2294 Dvr F Connolly No. 2 A.M.T. Coy att. 6th Field Amb.) and the orderly No. 9806 Pte. S Brew 6th Field Amb. were just about to commence their midday meal when an enemy shell exploded 5 yards from the car. The driver was standing just in front of the car & the orderly had stepped into the car to get his mess utensils when the shell exploded, the driver was killed instantly & the orderly severely wounded (sh.wd avulsed right arm sh. wd right knee, right foot). He died at No. 55 CCS on 16th & was buried at Daours Communal Cemetery Extension.

(Avulsed – a partial or complete tearing away of skin and tissue.)

There would definitely have been German soldiers among those treated by the 6th Field Ambulance, those it 'succoured', but Brew's inscription does give a slightly misleading idea of the exact circumstances of his death.

Samuel Brew was born in Britain, in Great Crosby near Liverpool. He emigrated to Australia in 1899 when he was twenty-three. His brother, Henry, also went to Australia, as did another brother, John. John served with the 38th Battalion Australian Infantry and was killed in action on 8 June 1917. He is commemorated on the Menin Gate. A cousin, Lieutenant Thomas Brew, was killed in action on 4 October 1917.

HE MADE THE GREAT SACRIFICE
MY ONLY SON

LANCE CORPORAL SIDNEY J CLEGG
LONDON REGIMENT (ROYAL FUSILIERS)
DIED 21 AUGUST 1918 AGED 22
BURIED GOMMECOURT BRITISH CEMETERY NO. 2, FRANCE

There is a large painting in St Mildred's Church, Whippingham on the Isle of Wight, which shows a dead British officer stretched out on a battlefield, one hand resting on the foot of a ghostly figure of the crucified Christ, hanging from the cross above him. The painting is called The Great Sacrifice, and the symbolism is clear: those who died for Britain sacrificed themselves for the world, in the same way that Christ had done.

Painted by James Clark (1858–1943) in 1914, 'The Great Sacrifice' was sold to raise money for a war relief charity. Queen Mary bought the painting and gave it to her husband's aunt, Princess Beatrice, whose son, Prince Maurice of Battenberg, George V's cousin, had been killed on 27 October 1914.

The painting shows an extremely unrealistic battlefield, but the image proved very consoling to the bereaved. The Daily Sketch produced it as a print for their Christmas 1914 edition. Framed prints can still be found hung beside the Roll of Honour in churches. The painting was also the inspiration for several stained glass war memorial windows.

In 1911, fifteen-year-old Sidney Clegg was a coal merchant's clerk living with his mother and step-father, his seventeen-year-old sister, Violet, and their four-year-old step-sister, Ivy. He served with the 1st Battalion London Regiment (Royal Fusiliers) but was posted to the 13th Battalion in time for their attack southwest of Bucquoy on 21 August 1918 in which he and two other soldiers of the battalion were killed.

SHOULD I FALL, GRIEVE NOT
I SHALL BE ONE WITH THE SUN
WIND AND FLOWERS

GUNNER HENRY JAMES BEZER
AUSTRALIAN FIELD ARTILLERY
DIED 22 AUGUST 1918 AGED 21
BURIED VILLERS-BRETONNEUX MILITARY CEMETERY, FRANCE

In one of his last letters home, the poet Sergeant Leslie Coulson reassured his father: 'If I fall do not grieve for me, I shall be one with the wind and sun and the flowers'. The words were reproduced in the preface to a book of Coulson's poetry, which his father published in 1917. The book achieved world-wide sales, which explains how Gunner Bezer's father in Australia became aware of the words.

Henry Bezer was a twenty-year-old wool-classer from Goulburn in New South Wales when he enlisted in September 1916. He served with the 7th Brigade Australian Field Artillery and was killed in action early on 22 August 1918. A witness described him to the Australian Red Cross Wounded and Missing Enquiry Bureau as:

> about 6 ft high, well built, fair complexion, brown hair, had a mole on the right cheek, full jovial round face, aged about 22. Came from the country, thought to have been a farmer.

Another witness related what happened:

> Informant states that they both belonged to the 107th Howitzer Battery. On 22/8/18 the Battery was in action at a place called by the boys 'Happy Valley' not far away from Bray. About half past 4 or 5 am just after the action started Bezer was killed outright by a shell, while he and Informant were working the gun to which they both belonged. Informant was right alongside him at the time and yet was not touched.

VILLERS-BRETONNEUX
CEMETERY

"TRUE GLORY
LIES IN NOBLE DEEDS"
CICERO

CAPTAIN WILLIAM JOHN ARMSTRONG PRATT MC
THE KING'S LIVERPOOL REGIMENT
DIED 23 AUGUST 1918 AGED 28
BURIED DOUCHY-LES-AYETTE BRITISH CEMETERY, FRANCE

Three days after Julius Caesar's assassination, Cicero attacked the consuls Mark Anthony and Dolabella:

> ... it is impossible for me to keep silence respecting the error into which you are both falling; for I believe that you, being both men of high birth, entertaining lofty views, have been eager to acquire, not money, as some too credulous people suspect, a thing which has at all times been scorned by every honourable and illustrious man, nor power procured by violence and authority such as never ought to be endured by the Roman people, but the affection of your fellow citizens, and glory. But glory is praise for deeds which have been done, and the fame earned by great services to the republic; which is approved by the testimony borne in its favour, not only by every virtuous man, but also by the multitude.
>
> *Philippics 1. 12.29*

Cicero does not mention the word 'noble' but the implication is that noble deeds are those that give great service to the state, as Captain Pratt's family believed he had done.

William John Armstrong Pratt was the son of Robert and Elizabeth Margaret Pratt. Born in Queen's County, Ireland, he was a journalist in Dublin before the outbreak of war. He served with the King's Liverpool Regiment and was killed in action during the Third Battle of Albert on 23 August 1918. Three months after his death the London Gazette published the citation for his Military Cross:

> For conspicuous gallantry and devotion to duty during a raid. He showed great pluck and dash as a company commander, and set a splendid example to his men, being one of the first to enter the enemy line. For three nights previously he had reconnoitred the ground.

HIS LAST WORDS AT HOME WERE "I SHALL BE ALRIGHT MOTHER"

PRIVATE PERCY COLE
LINCOLNSHIRE REGIMENT
DIED 23 AUGUST 1918 AGED 19
BURIED BAGNEUX BRITISH CEMETERY, FRANCE

You can imagine the scene at 33 Maple Road, Blackheath, Birmingham as Percy Cole prepared to leave for the front: his mother Mrs Ellen Cole fussing and fretting and her son trying to reassure her – 'I shall be alright mother'. He wasn't, and the fact that Cole's parents used these last words as his inscription shows how much they haunted them.

Percy Cole served with the 1st Battalion Lincolnshire Regiment, part of the 21st Division. On 20 August 1918 the battalion was in the trenches at Mailly Maillet when it was ordered to take up positions for an attack towards Beaucourt and the River Ancre. At 5.45 am on the 21st the battalion moved forward to its assembly position, the early morning mist being so dense that the planned smoke barrage designed to conceal their movement was cancelled. By the evening the battalion had reached the Ancre. Cole was among the wounded. He died two days later in a Casualty Clearing Station at Gezaincourt, 30 km from Beaucourt.

CABARET ROUGE
BRITISH CEMETERY

REMEMBER, WHATEVER HAPPENS
IT WILL HAVE BEEN
WORTH WHILE

LIEUTENANT ARTHUR GRANVILLE SHARP MC
ROYAL FIELD ARTILLERY
DIED 23 AUGUST 1918 AGED 20
BURIED CABARET ROUGE BRITISH CEMETERY, SOUCHEZ, FRANCE

Arthur Sharp was born in South Africa on 27 October 1897. On 24 October 1914 he enlisted in Thring's Horse, the 5th South African Mounted Brigade. He was just three days short of his seventeenth birthday.

To some Boers, Britain's war with Germany was South Africa's chance for freedom. What they had failed to achieve in the South African Wars at the beginning of the century could be achieved by siding with the Germans. To this end, General Manie Maritz issued a proclamation declaring the independence of the former South African Republic, Orange Free State, Cape Province and Natal.

Thring's Horse took part in the suppression of this nascent rebellion, which was more or less over by the time Sharp joined them. He transferred almost immediately to the 1st Mounted Brigade and took an active part in the German South-West African Campaign. On 1 December 1915 he was commissioned into the British Army, being gazetted a second lieutenant in the Royal Field Artillery. He joined D Battery in June 1916 and served with it in France, Belgium and Italy until his death in action on 23 August 1918. This was the same action for which he was awarded a Military Cross.

> On 23rd August 1918, near Hamelincourt, as forward observation officer, this officer showed conspicuous gallantry and devotion to duty. Under heavy fire for many hours, he continuously kept touch with the situation, and sent back most valuable reports. At one time he, with two signallers, was isolated between the front line flank companies of two battalions. He succeeded in sending back quickly and accurately the position of that flank, and the gap was filled.
> *London Gazette,* 1 February 1919

Sharp's mother chose his inscription, indicating the spirit in which her son entered the war and of how she sought consolation for his loss.

SON OF GEORGE SOMES LAYARD
"ENAMOURED OF LIFE
HE WENT LAUGHING
INTO THE ARMS OF DEATH"

LIEUTENANT PETER CLEMENT LAYARD
SUFFOLK REGIMENT
DIED 23 AUGUST 1918 AGED 22
BURIED DOUCHY-LES-AYETTE BRITISH CEMETERY, FRANCE

George Somes Layard (1857-1925), barrister and writer, wrote a memoir of his son, *Peter Clement Layard Extracts from His Letters*, from which he took his inscription:

> I do not claim for him that he was any more remarkable, and better, more
> heroic than hundreds of his fellows. Certainly he would not have claimed
> anything of the sort for himself, and would have laughed to scorn his
> fellow-officer's description of him as 'a great soldier'. And yet, like many
> more, enamoured of life he went laughing into the arms of death.

Layard enlisted on the outbreak of war. Commissioned in November 1914, he went to France with his regiment in January 1916. Badly wounded that June, he returned to the front in June 1918 and was killed two months later. A brother officer told to his parents:

> We were attacking Goniecourt on 23rd August, and the attack was
> extremely successful, and we were consolidating the positions won; your
> son was carrying on with the re-organization of his platoon. He went
> back to see if he could find any more men, and on his way back he
> came across a wounded Boche, whom he bound up and was talking to
> when he was hit through the heart by a sniper.

One of Layard's masters at Bedales summed up his attitude to life:

> Well, the war seized him, along with many others who would never
> have voluntarily chosen soldiering as an occupation; but I feel sure
> that Peter never had any regrets. It was life, and exciting and thrilling,
> and he would never worry himself about possibilities or what might
> have been.

"EVERY BUDDY'S BUDDY"

PRIVATE PETER HISLOP
MACHINE GUN CORPS
DIED 23 AUGUST 1918 AGED 35
BURIED RAILWAY CUTTING CEMETERY, COURCELLES-LE-COMTE, FRANCE

Do the quotation marks mean that this is what everybody said about Peter Hislop or is it a quotation from a popular song written in America in 1920? The last headstones were not erected in Railway Cutting Cemetery until 1925 so Hislop's younger brother, David, who chose the inscription, could easily have heard the song. Did he recognise his brother in the chorus?

> Buddy, he was everybody's buddy from the time he was a kid.
> He'd get the coal, chop the wood,
> He'd even run errands for the neighbourhood.
> Buddy, he would help the kids to study, he was everybody's friend.
> One day the angels in the heavens above
> Found out they needed someone up there to love;
> They called for Buddy, our Buddy
> I wish they'd send him home again.

Hislop, born and brought up in Glasgow, was a clerk before the war. He served with the 3rd Battalion Machine Gun Corps and was killed in action in the capture of Goniecourt on 23 August 1918. Two men from the battalion were taken prisoner and had an interesting story to tell:

> We tried to take our wounded with us, but a 'Hun' officer refused to let us get them all. This officer started beating one of the Gordons with a stick and told him to hurry up. He said he was going to shoot the two machine gunners because they had inflicted heavy casualties on German troops. At that moment a German Colonel appeared who was exceedingly nice to us and ordered us to take our wounded with us under escort to Achiet-le-Grand. He said we and the Gordons were brave fellows. ... [Advancing British soldiers rescued the prisoners and took their captors captive.] .... On going back to our own lines we told the K.R.Rs. 37th Division about the officer who had beaten the Gordon with the stick; the K.R.Rs. then bayonetted the officer.

ETERNAL REST
GOD GRANT TO YOUR SOUL
MY OWN DEAR DARLING BOY
FROM FATHER

SERJEANT PATRICK WALSH MM
GRENADIER GUARDS
DIED 23 AUGUST 1918 AGED 26
BURIED DOUCHY-LES-AYETTE BRITISH CEMETERY, FRANCE

Patrick Walsh came from Killinick, County Wexford and served, not with an Irish regiment, but with the Grenadier Guards. The position of Irish soldiers who served in the British Army, whether in Irish or English regiments, is illustrated by the fact that it was not until June 2013 that a memorial was commissioned in Ireland to the more than eight hundred Wexford men who lost their lives in the First World War. In announcing it, the Mayor of Wexford said that he knew it would be controversial in some places but that time had moved on, 'these people left Wexford in good faith and deserve to be commemorated'.

Walsh enlisted in the Grenadier Guards early in the war and went to France with the 3rd Battalion on 26 July 1915. The battalion served in France and Belgium throughout the war, taking part in all the major campaigns during which Walsh rose to the rank of serjeant and was awarded a Military Medal. He was killed in the Guards' attack on Boiry Becquerelle, Boyelle and Hamelincourt on 23 August 1918.

The first two lines of Walsh's inscription suggest that he was a Roman Catholic, a fact confirmed by the Irish census, which unlike the British census, asked people to state their religion. The last two lines express a tenderness between father and son that is relatively unusual among personal inscriptions.

SOLDAT SANS PEUR
ET SANS REPROCHE
TOMBÉ SUR LE CHAMP D'HONNEUR

CAPTAIN HAROLD BURKE MC
AUSTRALIAN INFANTRY
DIED 23 AUGUST 1918 AGED 23
BURIED CERISY-GAILLY MILITARY CEMETERY, FRANCE

He was advancing with coy H.Q. on the left of E-W road in front of Peronne; turning to give an order for the coy to advance, a 60 pr shell came over killing him outright and wounding several others. The head was almost severed from the body and he was taken back by S/B and buried near Hamel. ... He was one of the very bravest and best and most popular. He had a sister in the A.A.N.S. and a brother in the Artillery.
L/C Jackson 7.10.1918 Witness to the Australian Red Cross Wounded and Missing Enquiry Bureau

Burke's inscription references two of France's most respected soldiers, Pierre du Terrail (1476–1524), known as the Chevalier de Bayard, 'le chevalier sans peur et sans reproche', the knight without fear and beyond reproach, a reputation earned by his courage and his chivalrous behaviour, and Théophile Malo (1743–1800). Malo was a modest but effective soldier named by Napoleon as the 'first grenadier of France'. When he failed to answer his name at roll call his comrades replied, 'Tombé sur le champ d'honneur', fallen on the field of honour. For many years it was the custom in certain French Grenadier regiments for his name to be included in the roll call and for the oldest sergeant to shout out in reply, 'Tombé sur le champ d'honneur'.

Burke enlisted as a private on 15 August 1914. He served on Gallipoli and rose rapidly through the ranks until he was commissioned in September 1915. His Military Cross citation reads:

Under heavy shelling, this officer, regardless of any danger to himself, re-organised the right flank of the Battalion in the absence of the leading Company Commander who had been wounded. At a critical moment he reorganised men of another Battalion who were in the rear and sent them forward to their objective, and established a Strong Point in a sound tactical position under heavy fire. At all times he displayed cool judgment and sound leadership.

"STEEL TRUE AND BLADE STRAIGHT
THE GREAT ARTIFICER
MADE MY MATE"

LANCE CORPORAL GUY MELVILLE FARNDEN
ROYAL INNISKILLING FUSILIERS
DIED 23 AUGUST 1918 AGED 34
BURIED MONT NOIR MILITARY CEMETERY, ST JANS-CAPPEL, FRANCE

Trusty, dusky, vivid, true,
With eyes of gold and bramble-dew,
Steel-true and blade-straight,
The great artificer
Made my mate.

Honour, anger, valour, fire;
A love that life could never tire,
Death quench or evil stir,
The mighty master
Gave to her.

Teacher, tender, comrade, wife,
A fellow-farer true through life,
Heart-whole and soul free
The august father
Gave to me.
My Wife Robert Louis Stevenson (1850–1894)

Guy Farnden's wife, Edith, chose his inscription, transferring the qualities Stevenson had bestowed on his beloved wife onto her own husband to whom she had been married for ten years.

When the war broke out, Farnden was managing a boot shop. He originally served in the Royal Fusiliers before being transferred to the 1st Battalion Royal Inniskilling Fusiliers. The battalion were in the front line on the day he was killed, the war diary reporting: 'At 11.30 pm Boche deliver a counter attack on Brigade front and put down a Heavy Barrage on CT where parties were working'. The attack killed thirteen members of the battalion, wounded twenty-four and gassed fourteen.

THOU O'ER LOOK'ST THE TUMULT FROM AFAR AND SMILEST KNOWING ALL IS WELL

SECOND LIEUTENANT ROBERT CHARLES EVANS
WELSH REGIMENT
DIED 24 AUGUST 1918 AGED 36
BURIED POZIÈRES BRITISH CEMETERY, FRANCE

Tennyson is the most popular nineteenth-century poet quoted in personal inscriptions on British First World War headstones, and *In Memoriam AHH* is the most popular of his poems. Robert Evans' inscription comes from Canto CXXVII, which begins:

> And all is well, tho' faith and form
> Be sunder'd in the night of fear.

The stanza goes on to describe an apocalyptic scene before asserting that even in the midst of all this chaos, even while 'compass'd by the fires of Hell',

> Thou, dear spirit, happy star
> O'erlook'st the tumult from afar
> And smilest, knowing all is well.

Tennyson wrote the poem in memory of his friend, Arthur Hallam, who died suddenly in Vienna in 1833 at the age of twenty-two.

Robert Evans was a solicitor, in practice in his father's firm W.R. Evans, Lloyd and Evans of Wrexham. In November 1914 he enlisted as a private in the Royal Welch Fusiliers and was commissioned into the 15th Battalion Welsh Regiment in March 1917. On 24 August 1918, he was shot dead by a German prisoner near Thiepval. Evan's wife, Mrs Edith Lloyd Evans chose her husband's inscription. Two months after his death she had a son, whom she named Robert Charles after her husband.

SCHOLAR, POET, ORATOR
JUSTIFIED BY FAITH
IN JESUS CHRIST

LIEUTENANT COLONEL JOHN HAY MAITLAND HARDYMAN DSO MC
SOMERSET LIGHT INFANTRY
DIED 24 AUGUST 1918 AGED 23
BURIED BIENVILLERS MILITARY CEMETERY, FRANCE

Look again at John Hardyman's age and at his rank. Aged twenty-three he was a lieutenant colonel despite the fact that he had only joined the army in August 1914.

George Hardyman chose his son's inscription but apparently it was not the epitaph his son would have wanted. John Hardyman was a scholar; he won an open scholarship to Edinburgh University in 1911. He was a poet – a volume of his verse, A Challenge, was published in 1919. The reference to 'orator' will be a reference to the fact that Hardyman was a member of the council, and a keen advocate, of the Union for Democratic Control. Although not yet the pacifist organization that it became in the 1920s, the Union was regularly accused of undermining the war effort. Among its members were E.D. Morel, Norman Angell, Bertrand Russell, Ramsay MacDonald, all well-known opponents of war, and John Hay Maitland Hardyman, a lieutenant in the British Army in 1916, promoted captain and then major in April 1917, awarded a Military Cross in July 1916, promoted lieutenant colonel in May 1918, awarded a DSO on 11 August 1918 and killed in action on the 24th.

How did he square his beliefs with his military career? According his friend, Norman Hugh Romanes:

> He always professed strongly that his actions were absolutely consistent with his beliefs. While admiring the moral courage of many conscientious objectors, he was convinced that their attitude as a whole was tantamount to a refusal of the Cross.

A fervent Christian, as the second part of his inscription makes clear, Hardyman's poem, On Leave, expressed his belief, 'That through sacrifice the soul must grow'.

So what was the epitaph Hardyman would have chosen for himself? According to Romanes it would have ended as follows: 'He died as he lived, fighting for abstract principles in a cause which he did not believe in.'

FAIS CE QUE DOIS
ADVIENNE QUE POURRA

CAPTAIN LUDOVIC HEATHCOT-AMORY
ROYAL 1ST DEVON YEOMANRY
DIED 25 AUGUST 1918 AGED 37
BURIED DAOURS COMMUNAL CEMETERY EXTENSION, FRANCE

This is an ancient French proverb, which translates as 'Do your duty come what may' or, less formally, 'Do what you must whatever the results'.

On 24 August 1918, Captain Amory, as he was generally known, was serving on the Staff of the 32nd Division. That evening a German aeroplane bombed their Headquarters. Amory died of wounds a few hours later.

Amory's wartime diary survived and has been published in *Artillery and Trench Mortar Memories – 32nd Division*, edited by R. Whinyates. Here a friend describes him in the foreword as being 'characteristic of the best type of Englishman, no man more happy in temperament, more genuinely friendly in disposition'. The friend mentions particularly that Amory was always anxious to 'carry out his duties to the utmost of his ability'.

Amory's wife, Mary, chose his inscription. The proverb is not meant to be fatalistic, just utterly pragmatic – do your duty come what may. But Mary Heathcoat-Amory could never have guessed what was to come. She and her husband had three sons; Michael, the second son, was killed in an air crash in 1936; Patrick, the eldest, was killed at El Alamein in 1942; and Edgar was killed in Normandy on 23 June 1944. Patrick is commemorated on the Alamein Memorial, Edgar is buried in Ranville War Cemetery. His inscription reads:

> Fais ce que dois
> Advienne que pourra

SLEEP LIGHTLY, LAD THOU ART KING'S GUARD AT DAYBREAK

LIEUTENANT WILLIAM GODFREY CHARLTON
DURHAM LIGHT INFANTRY
DIED 26 AUGUST 1918 AGED 20
BURIED WARLENCOURT BRITISH CEMETERY, FRANCE

This inscription seems to be peculiarly geographic in its usage. In November 1917 the Rev. Ernest F.H. Capey wrote in *The United Methodist* of going for a walk to the church in Ford, Northumberland:

> On the inner door was suspended an artistic card *in memoriam* of the
> brave boys of the village who had lost their lives in the war. It was headed:
> Fought and died for Freedom:
> Sleep lightly, Lad,
> Thou art for King's Guard at daybreak;
> With spotless kit turn out,
> And take a place of honour.

A year earlier, the same verse appeared on the Roll of Honour in St Luke's Chapel at the Royal Victoria Infirmary, Newcastle-upon-Tyne. The *Newcastle Journal* reported that it was 'the work of Mr J.H. Binks of Ford', 'chastely and ably done', 'delicately executed, the gift of an anonymous friend'.

The North East War Memorial Project records several places where 'Sleep lightly lad thou art for King's guard at daybreak' is used as a war memorial inscription. None of these places is more than twelve miles from Newcastle.

William Charlton came from Seaton Delaval, nine miles from Newcastle. His father, John Charlton, chose his inscription. It is not the dedication on the Seaton Delaval memorial. This was unveiled on 2 September 1922 by Mr John Charlton 'whose two sons were killed in the war'. And what is the personal inscription on the headstone of his second son, Captain George Fenwick Hedley Charlton, South Wales Borderers, killed in action on 6 October 1916?

> Sleep lightly, Lad
> Thou art King's Guard
> At daybreak.

THEN THE GODS PITIED HIM
AND TOOK HIM TO THEIR MIDST

PRIVATE ARTHUR PROUT
AUSTRALIAN INFANTRY
DIED 26 AUGUST 1918 AGED 22
BURIED DIVE COPSE BRITISH CEMETERY, FRANCE

Who dies in youth and vigour dies the best.
Iliad Bk viii, 1.371 Homer

He whom the gods love dies young.
Hypsaeus

"Whom the gods love die young," was said of yore,
And many deaths do they escape by this:
The death of friends, and that which slays even more,
The death of friendship, love, youth, all that is,
Except mere breath.
Don Juan (Canto iv st.12) Byron

I would sooner see any of you struck down in the flower of youth than living on to lose, long before death comes, all that makes life worth living. Better death a thousand times, than gradual decay of mind and spirit; better death than faithlessness, indifference and uncleanness.
The Hill (1905) Horace Vachell

They shall grow not old, as we that are left grow old:
Age shall not weary them, nor the years condemn.
For the Fallen (1914) Laurence Binyon

Back through time, those who died young were the fortunate ones, the ones who would be young forever, hence Mrs Jessie Prout's choice of inscription for her son. Arthur Prout was twenty-two when he died of wounds on the Somme. His mother asked the Australian Red Cross for information about his death and was told:

> This man was admitted to a dressing station administered by this Field Ambulance on the Bray Corbie Road ... suffering from Bullet wound skull – fracture, and died a few minutes after admission.

TO END ALL WARS

PRIVATE HERBERT JOHN MARTIN
LONDON REGIMENT (ROYAL FUSILIERS)
DIED 27 AUGUST 1918 AGED 27
BURIED PÉRONNE ROAD CEMETERY, FRANCE

To Josiah James and Mary Annie Martin their son had died in the war to end all wars. The phrase owed its origins to a book by H.G. Wells, published in late 1914, titled *The War That Will End War*. And how was it going to do this? By smashing German militarism.

> We are fighting Germany ... we have to destroy an evil system of government and the mental and material corruption that has got hold of the German imagination and taken possession of German life. We have to smash Prussian Imperialism [which] has been for forty years an intolerable nuisance in the earth. Ever since the crushing of the French in 1871 the evil thing has grown and cast its spreading shadow over Europe. Germany has preached a propaganda of ruthless force and political materialism to the whole uneasy world. "Blood and iron," she boasted, was the cement of her unity, and almost as openly the little, mean, aggressive statesmen and professors who have guided her destinies to this present conflict have professed cynicism and an utter disregard of any ends but nationally selfish ends, as though it were religion.

But as Wells warned:

> There can be no diplomatic settlement that will leave German Imperialism free to explain away its failure to its people and start new preparations. We have to go on until we are absolutely done for, or until the Germans as a people know that they are beaten, and are convinced that they have had enough of war.

And that of course did not happen, at least not until 1945. But even then – 'Only the dead have seen the end of war': George Santayana 1922.

Herbert Martin, a commercial clerk at the time of the 1911 census, was the son of a bricklayer who lived in Woodford Green, London. He served first with the 5th Battalion London Regiment (Royal Fusiliers) but at the time of his death was with the 3rd.

HE TRIED TO DO HIS DUTY

PRIVATE HARRY RUSHWORTH
KING'S OWN ROYAL LANCASTER REGIMENT
DIED 29 AUGUST 1918 AGED 18
BURIED MORY STREET MILITARY CEMETERY, FRANCE

This is a very famous inscription, famous not because it belonged to Harry Rushworth but because it is carved on the grave of one of Victorian England's heroes, Sir Henry Lawrence (1806–1857).

Lawrence was the Chief Commissioner of Oudh when the Indian Rebellion broke out in May 1857. On the 30 June the residency at Lucknow came under siege from the rebels. In its grounds were more than 1,280 civilians gathered there for protection, many of them women and children. Lawrence tried to organise the defence with the 1,700 British and Indian soldiers and civilian volunteers he had at his disposal. However, on 2 July he was badly wounded by a shell. As he lay dying he said, 'Put on my tomb only this; Here lies Henry Lawrence who tried to do his duty'.

As was the way with 'heroic' Victorian deaths, the death scene and Lawrence's dying words became famous, especially as they echoed the dying words of another great nineteenth-century hero, Admiral Lord Nelson, which were either 'Kiss me Hardy' or 'Thank God I have done my duty'; no one is quite sure which way round he said them.

Lawrence's tombstone in St Mary's churchyard Lucknow reads:

> Here lies Henry Lawrence
> Who tried to do his duty
> May God have mercy on his soul

Sir Henry Lawrence was a fifty-one-year-old soldier and statesman born into a military family in India. Harry Rushworth was an eighteen-year-old boy whose father was an engine driver in Huddersfield. But 'duty' was an obligation they both felt. Rushworth served with 'C' Company 8th Battalion King's Own Royal Lancaster Regiment and was killed near Ecoust. As the Germans withdrew in front of the British advance they left behind teams of machine gunners hidden in the folds of the rough terrain who wrought havoc on the advancing British. Rushworth was one of the many casualties.

INDIAN TRIBE 6 NATIONS
DIED FOR HONOUR OF EMPIRE
EVER REMEMBERED
BY WIFE AND CHILDREN

SAPPER LEWIS WILSON
CANADIAN ENGINEERS
DIED 31 AUGUST 1918 AGED 38
BURIED AUBIGNY COMMUNAL CEMETERY EXTENSION, FRANCE

Sapper Wilson was a First Nation American Indian: a member of the 6 Nations Tribe. Many Dominion Governments were reluctant to arm and train their indigenous people. New Zealand only envisaged Maoris in non-combatant roles; Australia was reluctant to enlist Aborigines at all. The Canadian Government too was initially reluctant, this despite the fact that many of the Indian tribes were very keen to join up, and many of them were already serving in militia units.

Timothy C. Winegard's book, Indigenous Peoples of the *British Dominions and the First World War*, explains why this was so. Money, employment and adventure all played their part, as they did with all recruits of whatever nationality. But, in addition, many North American Indians were keen to revive the warrior tradition of their ancestors, feeling these had stagnated after years of living on the reserves and of being on the receiving end of Western schooling and religious education.

However, whilst many North American Indians were willing to put their warrior heritage at the service of the British Crown, it was the British Crown they wanted to serve rather than the Dominion Government. The way was opened for them after October 1915 when the British Government made a direct appeal for the recruitment of indigenous people.

All this fits Lewis Wilson precisely. His inscription asserts his race. He had already served three years with a militia unit, the Haldimand Rifles, and his wife states specifically that he 'Died for the honour of the British Empire'.

Wilson served in the 3rd Battalion Canadian Engineers. On 30 August 1918 they were engaged in work on a tramway running from Beaurains and Neuville Vitasse to Wancourt. That night an 'E.A. bomb' fell on their billets, killing two soldiers and wounding seven others. Wilson died the next day in a Casualty Clearing Station in Aubigny-en-Artois.

HIS MEN WROTE ON ROUGH CROSS "IN MEMORY OF A VERY BRAVE BRITISH OFFICER"

SECOND LIEUTENANT LAMONT LIVINGSTONE PATERSON
LONDON REGIMENT (POST OFFICE RIFLES)
DIED 1 SEPTEMBER 1918 AGED 24
BURIED GUARDS CEMETERY, COMBLES, FRANCE

This 'very brave British officer' was Canadian born and bred, as his father had been before him. A graduate of Manitoba University, Lamont was a law student with the firm of Richards and Sweatman when he enlisted on 16 May 1916. He served initially with the 196th (Western Universities) Battalion, which began a recruiting campaign in the universities of western Canada early in 1916.

Although the 196th tried to stay together once they arrived in Europe, the preponderance of university graduates within their ranks meant that the members became a ready source of officers. Paterson was commissioned into the 8th Battalion London Regiment (Post Office Rifles) on 1 January 1918. He was killed in action on 1 September 1918 during the Second Battle of Bapaume.

The men of his platoon created their own wooden cross, the rough cross of the inscription, to mark their officer's grave. To them he was British, which is how many Canadians at the time saw themselves – or perhaps even, 'better Britons'.

Lamont Paterson was the son of Judge George Paterson and his wife, Mrs Paterson. George Paterson died in 1923, the same year his son's body was exhumed and reburied in the Guard's Cemetery at Combles. It was Mrs Paterson therefore who chose her son's inscription. Lamont was her only child.

THE SUPREME SACRIFICE

CORPORAL ROBERT JAMES ANDREW
AUSTRALIAN INFANTRY
DIED 1 SEPTEMBER 1918 AGED 25
BURIED PÉRONNE COMMUNAL CEMETERY EXTENSION, FRANCE

Corporal Robert James Andrew was killed in action at the retaking of the summit of Mont St Quentin on 1 September 1918. The next day the Australian Infantry took Péronne. These were among the finest actions of the Australian forces during the whole war and their casualties were very high.

Corporal Andrew's wife instigated an Australian Red Cross Wounded and Missing Enquiry Bureau search for her husband. The results show how difficult it was to ascertain exactly what had happened to a casualty. The witnesses agree that, 'Andrew was from Victoria, tall, very thin, fair hair, about twenty-six years', but there is not much agreement about how he died.

- ○ 'I didn't see Andrew, who was a M/Gunner in my D.XV. killed instantly by a m.g.bullet through the head at Mont St Quentin about 4 pm.'
- ○ 'Andrews was in the trench waiting to go over when he was hit by a piece of shell and killed right out. I saw this. I don't know about burial as we were going on.'
- ○ 'He was killed with four others by a shell in the dugout … It happened about 4.10 pm before our hop over, and Fritz was busy strafing us at the time.'
- ○ 'I saw Morris D.Coy. S/B and Andrew D.XVI both killed instantly by the same shell alongside of me at Mont St Quentin about 6 pm in front line of trenches before the hop over.'
- ○ 'Casualty was advancing at Mont St Quentin when a machine gun bullet entered his side killing him instantly.'

Corporal Andrew's wife, Rhoda, used the title of Sir John Arkwright's famous poem, *The Supreme Sacrifice* for her husband's headstone inscription. The poem is much better known as the hymn *O Valiant Hearts*, which for many years used to be sung at Remembrance Services until its sentiments went out of fashion.

IN LOVING MEMORY
OF OUR ONLY CHILD
R.I.P.

SECOND LIEUTENANT JOHN GEORGE JOSEPH WILLIAMSON
ROYAL IRISH REGIMENT
DIED 2 SEPTEMBER 1918 AGED 19
BURIED DRANOUTRE MILITARY CEMETERY, BELGIUM

At 4 am on the 1st September orders were received to change direction
left and advance on Wulverghem ... The advance encountered no serious
opposition until the Kemmel-Neuve Eglise road was reached at 9 am.
Here the right of the battalion was held up by heavy machine gun and
trench mortar fire from the Neuve Eglise Ridge. Our trench mortars
were brought to bear on the German machine guns and silenced those
nearest the battalion. At 10.30 a forward movement was made, but B
Company lost all its officers, killed or wounded, the right platoon of C
Company lost 2nd Lieutenant Williamson killed and most of his men
either killed or wounded.
The Campaigns and History of the Royal Irish Regiment 1902–1922

There is no doubt at all that he was the best officer in the company,
and he was very popular with everyone. His men would have followed
him anywhere ... Whenever there was a difficulty, or an awkward job
had to be tackled with judgment or tact, I always knew that I could rely
on him to take it in hand and see it through properly.
Letter to Williamson's parents from his Commanding Officer

Williamson was the only child of George and Margaret Williamson of Dublin. Born,
brought up and educated in Ireland, Williamson went to RMC Sandhurst in May 1917,
was gazetted Second Lieutenant in the Royal Irish Regiment in April 1918, served with
them in France and Flanders from June 1918 and was killed in action at Wulverghem.

FOR YOUR TOMORROW
WE GAVE OUR TODAY

LIEUTENANT CHARLES ARNOLD GRANT
PRINCESS PATRICIA'S CANADIAN LIGHT INFANTRY
DIED 2 SEPTEMBER 1918 AGED 38
BURIED LIGNY-ST FLOCHEL BRITISH CEMETERY, AVERDOINGT, FRANCE

This inscription was written by J. Maxwell Edmonds, a Classics don at Cambridge, and included with eight other of his compositions in the 1919 HMSO publication, *Suggested Inscriptions for War Memorials*. Edmonds' words read:

> When you go home, tell them of us and say
> 'For your to-morrows, these gave their today'

The most famous use of this inscription is on the Kohima Memorial, which marks the point at which the Japanese advance into India was halted in April 1944. It is now often recited at Remembrance Day services, usually after the two minutes' silence.

Charles Grant's step-sister, Marjorie Grant, chose it. She was now the guardian of his son, Douglas James Grant, who was seven when his father was killed, Grant's wife and parents having died before he joined up.

Grant was a barrister, a partner in the firm of Parker, Grant, Freeman and Abbott, when he enlisted in December 1915. Badly wounded on the Somme in September 1916, which resulted in the amputation of the tip of the little finger on his right hand, he did not return to the front until early in 1917. He was wounded again less seriously in June 1917, and then again – 'Dangerously wounded g.s.w pelvis penetrating' – on 28 August 1918 in the Canadian action at Jigsaw Wood. He died five days later in a Casualty Clearing Station at Ligny-St Flochel where he is buried.

MORE BRAVE FOR THIS
THAT HE HATH MUCH TO LOVE

LIEUTENANT JAMES MCDONALD MC
CANADIAN INFANTRY
DIED 2 SEPTEMBER 1918 AGED 40
BURIED TIGRIS LANE CEMETERY, WANCOURT, FRANCE

James McDonald was a married man, which provides a clue to the inscription his wife chose. It comes from Wordsworth's *Character of the Happy Warrior*, which asks – 'Who is the happy warrior? Who is he that every man in arms would wish to be?' After enumerating the noble and honourable qualities that make a man a good soldier, Wordsworth adds that he –

> Is yet a Soul whose master-bias leans
> To homefelt pleasures and to gentle scenes;
> Sweet images! which, whereso'er he be,
> Are at his heart; and such fidelity
> It is his darling passion to approve;
> More brave for this, that he hath much to love.

'Much to love' meant that these men had much to lose, explaining why, to Wordsworth, they were 'more brave' than single men.

James McDonald, born in Morayshire, Scotland in 1878, enlisted in Vancouver, British Columbia in 1915 and served in France with the 72nd Battalion Canadian Infantry from August 1916. He was killed in action on the day Canadian and British forces took the Drocourt-Quéant Line. This was the same day that he won his Military Cross:

> 72nd Battalion Canadian Infantry War Diary
> In the Trenches 2 September 1918
> The Battn went over on a 500 yd front at 5 am. The barrage which was on a three division front was perfect and very accurate. By 7.20 am all objectives were taken and the battalion was establishing itself in the Red Line. 6 officers [German] (including 3 M.O.s) and 445 other ranks were taken prisoners. Up to taking of our first objective our casualties were light but when advancing to the Red Line we met intense M.G. fire from our left flank. Major A.V. Wood MC and Lieut. J. McDonald were killed ...

BROTHER OF EMMANUEL GOLDSTEIN KILLED IN ACTION 25 SEPTEMBER 1918

RIFLEMAN BENJAMIN GOLDSTEIN
RIFLE BRIGADE
DIED 6 SEPTEMBER 1918 AGED 24
BURIED ABBEVILLE COMMUNAL CEMETERY EXTENSION, FRANCE

Benjamin and Emmanuel Goldstein were the sons of Morris and Milly Goldstein. Morris was born in Chachinow, Plotzk a town now in central Poland but at the time of his birth in Russia. The town had a huge, vibrant Jewish community, which was reduced to no more than a handful by the end of the Second World War. Morris's wife Milly, Amelia Bernberg, was born in Kuldiga, a town in western Latvia, where there had been a similarly thriving Jewish community. Many of the residents were German, which is how Milly identified her nationality in the 1911 British census.

Morris Goldstein, who was a tailor, came to Britain in 1896 when he was thirty-six, and became a naturalised British subject in December 1904. There is no evidence that Milly ever became a British subject. All their six children were born in Britain, of whom five survived to adulthood.

The three eldest boys all served in the British Army, Benjamin and Emmanuel, the second and third sons, both being killed in 1918 within twenty days of each other.

Morris Goldstein signed for Benjamin's inscription, whereas their eldest brother, Samuel, signed for Emmanuel's:

> Brother of Ben Goldstein
> Died of wounds Sept. 6th 1918.

By this time Samuel Reuben Goldstein was calling himself Stanley Robert Golding. Later, the youngest brother, Louis, also changed his surname to Golding. It was a sign that the brothers wanted to assimilate themselves seamlessly into British society. But it was also an indication that they felt a change of name was necessary to achieve this.

ABBEVILLE COMMUNAL
CEMETERY

NATION WITH NATION
LAND WITH LAND
UNARMED SHALL LIVE
AS COMRADES FREE

PRIVATE ARTHUR EDMUND LATCHFORD
ROYAL ARMY MEDICAL CORPS
DIED 8 SEPTEMBER 1918 AGED 20
BURIED PÉRONNE COMMUNAL CEMETERY EXTENSION, FRANCE

This wonderful Utopian world where men will live at peace, guided by science and reason, where woman will be man's 'mate and peer' and art and music will blossom, is envisaged by John Addington Symonds in his poem, *The Vista* (1880). But it is more likely that Arthur Latchford's mother, who chose the inscription, knew the lines from a hymn, based on a shortened version of Symonds' poem.

Symonds, a literary critic and cultural historian, was a fairly controversial figure. An advocate of homosexuality, verging on pederasty, Symonds admired the Greek world where relationships between men and youths were not frowned on, and looked forward to a time when homosexuality would no longer be a sin. It is unlikely that Mrs Latchford was familiar with Symonds' writing, which is why the hymn is a more likely source. Called *These things shall be a loftier race*, Latchford's inscription comes from verse three, which is the same as verse seven of the poem:

> Nation with nation, land with land,
> Unarmed shall live as comrades free;
> In every heart and brain shall throb
> The pulse of one fraternity.

Arthur Latchford joined the army in October 1915. He served with the 38th Field Ambulance RAMC and was killed during the battle to take Guyencourt on 8 September 1918. The eldest child of William and Annie Latchford, of Boxmoor, Hertfordshire, he worked for the printers McCorquodale and Co Ltd, Milton Keynes, where his name appears on their war memorial.

SUCH A SLEEP THEY SLEEP
THE MEN I LOVED
R.I.P.

SECOND LIEUTENANT WILLIAM EDWARD GILLESPIE
RIFLE BRIGADE
DIED 11 SEPTEMBER 1918 AGED 28
BURIED GOUZEAUCOURT NEW BRITISH CEMETERY, FRANCE

After 'the last battle', the dying Arthur tells Sir Bedevere, 'the last of all his knights',

> The sequel of today unsolders all
> The goodliest fellowship of famous knights
> Whereof this world holds record. Such a sleep
> They sleep – the men I loved. I think that we
> Shall never more, at any future time,
> Delight our souls with talk of knightly deeds,
> Walking about the gardens and the halls
> Of Camelot, as in the days that were.
> *Morte d'Arthur* Tennyson

These haunting words will have resonated with many people who felt their lives could never be the same again now that their menfolk were dead. William Gillespie's mother chose his inscription. Her husband Denis had died in October 1915, her son William, was killed on 11 September 1918 and another son, Daniel, seven days later.

William, at the time of his death attached to the 12th Battalion London Regiment, was in the front line near Epehy on 11 September, the night the Germans put down a box barrage and attacked Tattenham Post. According to the war diary, 'D Coy were surrounded and the post taken'. Was this when Gillespie was killed? His body was discovered in an unmarked grave a year later.

Gillespie's older brother, Daniel, a Lance Corporal with the 58th Division Signal Company Royal Engineers, was killed on 18 September. One of his other brothers, a Mr J. Gillespie, chose this inscription. It comes from Shakespeare's *Macbeth*:

> After life's fitful fever
> He sleeps well.

AS YESTERDAY

PRIVATE ROBERT ILLTYD FRENCH
YORK AND LANCASTER REGIMENT
DIED 12 SEPTEMBER 1918
BURIED RUYAULCOURT MILITARY CEMETERY, FRANCE

Lord, thou hast been our dwelling place in all generations.
Before the mountains were brought forth, or ever thou hadst formed
the earth and the world, even from everlasting, thou art God.
Thou turnest man to destruction; and sayest, Return, ye children of men.
For a thousand ages in thy sight are but as yesterday when it is past,
and as a watch in the night.
Psalm 90

'For a thousand ages in thy sight are but as yesterday', or as it says in Isaac Watts'
beautiful hymn based on the same psalm: 'A thousand ages in thy sight are like an
evening gone'. Man's mortal life is but a fleeting moment in eternity, 'as yesterday', only
God is eternal, 'our shelter from the stormy blast, and our eternal home'.

Mrs Martha French chose the inscription for her son Robert, but her husband, another
Robert French, also died on active service. He was a time-expired naval petty officer who
re-joined the navy on the outbreak of war. He served on board HMS *Moldavia*, an armed
merchant cruiser on patrol in the North Sea and, according to the ship's logbook, died on
board ship 'from haemorrhage following cancer of the stomach'. His body was 'committed
to the deep' the following day.

There is not the same level of detail about Robert Illtyd French's death. He served in
France and Flanders from 17 April 1915 and at the time of his death was with the 2/4th
York and Lancaster Regiment, part of the 62nd Division. On the day French was killed,
the Division successfully took the town of Havrincourt, the first breach in the German
Hindenburg Line.

HE LOVED TO DO A KIND ACTION

SECOND LIEUTENANT HARLEY BENTHAM
DUKE OF WELLINGTON'S WEST RIDING REGIMENT
DIED 16 SEPTEMBER 1918 AGED 23
BURIED SUNKEN ROAD CEMETERY, BOISLEUX-ST MARC, FRANCE

Despite the stereotype, not all officers came from the privileged, moneyed classes. Harley Bentham was the son of a Midlands Railway Company signalman who began his working life as an assistant railway porter.

Bentham attended Giggleswick Grammar School and left to become a clerk in the Bank of Liverpool in Settle. In January 1916 he enlisted as a private in the Duke of Wellington's West Riding Regiment, was recommended for a commission in December and was gazetted second lieutenant the following August.

On 13 September 1918 Bentham was wounded in action by shellfire 'whilst gallantly leading his men' in the successful attack on Havrincourt, so the letter from his lieutenant colonel told his parents. He reassured them that their son had not suffered and that he had died shortly after reaching the Casualty Clearing Station. There's always a suspicion that such reassurances were mere words, especially as in Bentham's case we know that he did not die until three days later.

Thomas Bentham chose a very gentle inscription for his son, who was his parents' only child – 'He loved to do a kind action'. One such action was a letter he wrote to the sister of one of the men in his regiment. This was whilst he was still a private so it was not his duty to do so but as he told her:

> I have been asked by some of the lads to write to you and tell you
> how sorry we are and how we sympathise with you in your great loss.

Bentham told the sister how her brother had been killed when a shell burst on the parapet right beside him. He assured her that death would have been instantaneous and that he would not have suffered. In this instance it is possible Bentham was speaking the truth.

I MOURN FOR YOU IN SILENCE
BUT NOT WITH OUTWARD SHOW

LIEUTENANT WILLIAM CLARENCE MCGREGOR MC
AUSTRALIAN LIGHT INFANTRY
DIED 16 SEPTEMBER 1918 AGED 24
BURIED JEANCOURT COMMUNAL CEMETERY EXTENSION, FRANCE

William Clarence McGregor, a 'motor' driver, enlisted on 17 September 1914. The attestation form in his service file records that he was 21, born in Bellingen, New South Wales the son of Jessie and the late Dugald McGregor. The next paper in the file is a copy of this form stamped 'discharged'. Then there is another attestation form. This time for Albert Murray, a 'motor mechanic' who enlisted on 2 July 1915. Murray was 22, born in Auckland, New Zealand the son of Mr E Murray. The form asks: 'Have you ever been discharged from HM Forces?', 'Have you ever served in HM Forces?' and 'Have you ever been rejected as unfit?'. Murray's answer to all three was 'no'.

Commissioned in June 1916, Murray served with the 49th Battalion Australian Infantry. A month after being awarded a Military Cross for 'conspicuous daring', he was killed by machine-gun fire whilst out on patrol.

A year after Murray's death his mother wrote to the military authorities to say that, 'as the mother of the above-named soldier ... I desire to take the necessary steps to have his correct name recorded'.

> My son enlisted to leave with the first lot of men to go and was very disappointed when he contracted rheumatic fever and instead of sailing with his camp comrades he had to go into hospital for 9 weeks and as a consequence received his discharge. Later on when he considered that he had removed all trace of the [disease] he endeavoured to re-enlist but was advised that his former illness, which had to be disclosed, would come against him. Not to be defeated in this worthy object he enlisted in a name other than his own and sailed as if Lieut Albert Murray in the troopship Ayrshire in 1916 ...

Mrs McGregor succeeded, the name on her son's headstone reads: 'Lieutenant W.C. McGregor served as Albert Murray MC', the Commission insisting on the name 'Murray' so that his military identity was not lost. Her stoic inscription epitomes the view that private mourning was authentic grieving: 'I mourn for you in silence / But not with outward show / For those who mourn sincerely / Mourn silently and slow'.

MAN'S INHUMANITY TO MAN MAKES COUNTLESS THOUSANDS MOURN

LIEUTENANT ERNEST CECIL STEELE
MACHINE GUN CORPS
DIED 18 SEPTEMBER 1918 AGED 21
BURIED HEUDICOURT COMMUNAL CEMETERY EXTENSION, FRANCE

Ernest Steele's mother was German. She became a naturalised British citizen in 1894, the same year she married James Steele in London. It is not possible to determine the sort of relationship someone like Rosa Koehne would have had with her native country, nor how she would have felt when the two countries were at war, but perhaps the fact that her son was a volunteer is a clue.

Steele enlisted in the 16th London Regiment and went with it to France in August 1915. At eighteen he would have needed his parents' signed permission to do this. A year later he was commissioned into the Machine Gun Corps.

On 18 September 1918, the British launched an attack on Epehy, one of the outposts of the Hindenburg Line. Three hundred machine guns, together with a creeping barrage from 1500 artillery pieces, helped them to a small but significant victory in which Steele was killed.

Steele's father signed for his inscription. It comes from verse seven of *Man Was Made to Mourn* by Robert Burns (1759–1796):

> Many and sharp the num'rous ills
> Inwoven with our frame!
> More pointed still we make ourselves,
> Regret, remorse and shame!
> And man, whose heav'n-erected face
> The smiles of love adorn, –
> Man's inhumanity to man
> Makes countless thousands mourn!

The Steeles were not the only family to choose this inscription and the War Graves Commission, which had given itself the power to censor inscriptions, did not refuse to accept it – you were not allowed to insult the Germans, or the British for that matter, but you could criticise war.

WE ARE YOURS
ENGLAND, MY OWN!

SECOND LIEUTENANT THOMAS EDWARD LAWRENCE
ROYAL SUSSEX REGIMENT
DIED 22 SEPTEMBER 1918 AGED 19
BURIED DOINGT COMMUNAL CEMETERY EXTENSION, PÉRONNE, FRANCE

Thomas Lawrence was a fifteen-year-old schoolboy at Malvern College when the war broke out. Four years later, aged nineteen, he arrived in France on 31 July and seven weeks later he was dead. His sister chose his inscription from W.E. Henley's patriotic poem *England, My England*:

> What have I done for you,
> England, my England?
> What is there I would not do,
> England, my own?

The inscription comes from verse three:

> Ever the faith endures,
> England, my England: –
> 'Take and break us: we are yours,
> England my own!
> Life is good, and joys run high
> Between English earth and sky:
> Death is death; but we shall die
> To the song on your bugles blown,
> England –
> To the stars on your bugles blown!'

The poem expresses pride in English achievements: 'Where shall the watchful sun ... match the master-work you've done?'; a belief that England has a duty to guard the world: 'They call you proud and hard ... you with worlds to watch and ward', and a certainty that England is doing God's work: 'Chosen daughter of the Lord, spouse-in-chief of the ancient sword'. The refrain, which varies slightly from verse to verse, became a rallying cry of Empire: 'To the song on your bugles blown' ... 'round the world' ... 'down the years' ... 'to the stars' ... 'round the pit' ... 'out of heaven'.

BORN TO KNOW NOT
WINTER ONLY SPRING

SECOND LIEUTENANT SIR JOHN BRIDGER SHIFFNER
ROYAL SUSSEX REGIMENT
DIED 24 SEPTEMBER 1918 AGED 19
BURIED BELLICOURT BRITISH CEMETERY, FRANCE

Sir John Bridger Shiffner, 6th Baronet, had been at the front for two days when he was killed in action on the 24 September 1918, the day the 2nd Battalion Royal Sussex Regiment captured the high ground north of Gricourt. He survived this action but later that day the Germans counter-attacked with some four hundred men.

> Captain Roberts ordered his company to open fire on the advancing enemy and when they were within 30 yards, the leading waves began to waver, on seeing this, Captain Roberts ordered his men to fix bayonets and then to charge the enemy. The men all rose from their positions in shell holes and charged with the bayonet and utterly routed the enemy, taking over 40 prisoners ...This action ... was a fine example of the use of Infantry weapons and the value of the dash and fighting spirit shown by all ranks who took part, as their total number was less than 80, thus being out-numbered by 5 to 1.
> Battalion War Diary

Shiffner was killed in the bayonet charge. He was nineteen and had been married for six weeks. His younger brother, Henry, inherited the title and was killed in action in North Africa in 1941 aged thirty-nine. The Dowager Lady Shiffner, Sir John's mother, chose his inscription from Robert Louis Stevenson's (1850–1894) *In Memoriam F.A.S.* These are the first two verses:

> Yet, O stricken heart, remember, O remember
> How of human days he lived the better part.
> April came to bloom and never dim December
> Breathed its killing chills upon the head or heart.
>
> Doomed to know not Winter, only Spring, a being
> Trod the flowery April blithely for awhile,
> Took his fill of music, joy of thought and seeing,
> Came and stayed and went, nor ever ceased to smile.

GOD'S HUSBANDMAN THOU ART
IN HIS UNWITHERING SHEAVES
BIND MY HEART

DRIVER ALEXANDER APPLEBY
AUSTRALIAN FIELD ARTILLERY
DIED 25 SEPTEMBER 1918 AGED 28
BURIED ST SEVER CEMETERY EXTENSION, ROUEN, FRANCE

Driver Appleby's widow, Sarah, chose the final two lines of *Laus Mortis* – In Praise of Death – by Frederic Lawrence Knowles (1869-1905) for her husband's inscription. Why should we praise death? Because it 'gives us life, and in exchange takes breath'; because 'Life lends us only feet, Death gives us wings', and because in death, whether we 'wear a crown or bear a yoke' we will all be equal, 'when once your coverlet of grass is spread'. Life is the sower and death is the reaper: 'God's husbandman'. Death has traditionally been portrayed as the reaper; Knowles takes the analogy further and portrays the dead as gathered corn, bound in 'unwithering' sheaves close to God.

> – Thou waitest, Reaper lone,
> Until the multitudinous grain hath grown
> – Scythe-bearer, when thy blade
> Harvests my flesh, let me be unafraid!
> – God's husbandman thou art!
> In His unwithering sheaves, O bind my heart!

Appleby, who enlisted in March 1917, was a horse driver from Perth in Western Australia. He served as a driver in the 3rd Australian Field Artillery Brigade and died of wounds in hospital at Rouen.

STAND FAST CRAIGELLACHIE

SECOND LIEUTENANT ALEXANDER GRANT
GRENADIER GUARDS
DIED 27 SEPTEMBER 1918 AGED 19
BURIED SANDERS KEEP MILITARY CEMETERY, GRAINCOURT-LÈS-HAVRINCOURT, FRANCE

By choosing this motto for his only son, Alexander Grant established his kinship with Clan Grant whose motto and war cry this is. 'Stand fast' may be understood today as an instruction, but at one time it was a quality, a synonym for steadfast. To the Grants, Craigellachie, a hill with a commanding view of the Strathspey, is a symbol of strength and watchfulness; it is the place where beacons were lit to alert the community to danger – to the need to stand fast, and to be steadfast.

Alexander Grant left Eton in 1917 and took a commission in the 1st Battalion Grenadier Guards. He went to the front on 29 April 1918 and served continuously until he was killed in action on 27 September. This is the day the Guards crossed the Canal du Nord on the Hindenburg Line and took Sanders Keep, which gave its name to the cemetery where Grant is buried.

In announcing his death in *The Times*, Grant's father proudly quoted a letter from his son's captain:

> I had seen a good deal of his conduct during the morning, and every time I saw him he was smiling and cheerful, moving about and encouraging his platoon to do their utmost in a most difficult attack ... He died upholding the great traditions of his school and his regiment ... He was a true Grenadier, and understood the full meaning of *Vitai lampada traduit.*

Vitae lampada traduit – they hand on the torch of life – a phrase forever associated with Sir Henry Newbolt's poem *Vitai Lampada* where at a desperate moment in a battle it is the voice of a schoolboy who rallies the ranks with his cry of 'play up, play up and play the game'.

B.A. JESUS COLLEGE, CAMBRIDGE
SERVED AS
SECOND LIEUTENANT
13TH BN. MIDDLESEX REGIMENT

ERNEST GEORGE DE LATHOM HOPCRAFT
DIED 27 SEPTEMBER 1918 AGED 32
BURIED FLESQUIÈRES HILL BRITISH CEMETERY, FRANCE

Ernest Hopcraft died as a private in the London Regiment but unusually his headstone mentions neither, just the rank and the regiment in the inscription.

In April 1916, Second Lieutenant Ernest George de Lathom Hopcraft went to France with the 13th Battalion Middlesex Regiment where he acted as billeting officer. Some French people were reluctant to have British officers billeted on them and one woman in particular was very uncooperative. In an attempt to get Hopcraft out of her house she began hitting and slapping him ... and he retaliated. Hopcraft was arrested, court martialled and on 19 February 1917 dismissed from the service for 'committing an offence against the person of a resident'.

Despite appeals to the War Office, Hopcraft was not reinstated so he re-enlisted as a private, served in the London Regiment and was killed in action on 27 September 1918. A memorial plaque in All Saint's Church, Middleton Cheney, Northamptonshire told the story as his father wanted it to be known:

Ernest George de Lathom Hopcraft
Aged 32 years. The only son of Ernest Hopcraft J.P. Northants, of Brackley and Middleton Cheney. Who answered duty's call and volunteered and was given a Commission in the 13th Middlesex Regiment.
He gave his life, his all, for his King and Country.
After having fought in Palestine he fell in action at the assault on the German Hindenburg Line at Marcoing near Cambrai.
September 27th 1918; 5 weeks and 4 days before the Armistice.
Gone but never forgotten.
At the Battle of Flesquières near Marcoing he gallantly attacked, single handed a German machine gun post and was killed

Ironically, had Mr E. Hopcraft JP not used his son's headstone to draw attention to his disgrace no one would have sought out the story.

A BROKEN MELODY

PRIVATE JAMES BLENCOWE KEATING
TANKS CORPS
DIED 27 SEPTEMBER 1918 AGED 19
BURIED FLESQUIÈRES HILL BRITISH CEMETERY, FRANCE

In 1892 a musical play opened in London called *A Broken Melody*. Reviews were mixed: one pronounced it 'feeble, tedious and commonplace', but *The Times* declared the combination of music, acting and sentiment made it irresistible. *The London Daily News* attributed the play's success to its simple blend of pathos and humour, and to Auguste van Biene who played the leading role. Van Biene is thought to have performed the role more than 6,000 times before he died in 1913, and he and his wife also starred in the 1896 film version.

The play was so popular that it gave rise to a common figure of speech: 'a broken melody' became a term to describe something that ended abruptly when it had been expected to keep running sweetly along – just as James and Ida Spencer had expected their nineteen-year-old son's life would do. It meant an unforeseen end of an era, an interrupted life.

James Blencowe Keating was the only son of James Keating, a self-employed engraver from Middlesborough, and his wife Ida. He served originally with the Yorkshire Regiment before transferring to the 1st Gun Carrier Company, Tank Corps formed in November 1917. Gun carriers were tracked vehicles designed to carry 6" howitzers and sixty pounders over the battlefield behind the advancing infantry. However, by September 1918 these carriers were being used to transport ammunition and supplies, it being estimated that their carrying capacity was equal to that of 291 human porters.

Keating was killed in action on 27 September when the 3rd Division retook the village of Flesquières, lost to the Germans in November 1917, a key stage in the Allies' advance to victory.

WE IN SPIRIT
STILL LIVE, LOVE AND COMMUNE
WITH ALL ON EARTH
MOTHER

PRIVATE HARRY WALTER EVANS
CANADIAN INFANTRY
DIED 30 SEPTEMBER 1918 AGED 21
BURIED CANTIMPRÉ CANADIAN CEMETERY, SAILLY, FRANCE

Private Evans' inscription asserts his mother's belief in Spiritualism – the belief that the spirit never dies and that it is possible for humans to communicate across the chasm of death. While there were many cranks and charlatans among early twentieth-century Spiritualists, there were also many well known, respected people, among them Sir Arthur Conan Doyle author of the Sherlock Holmes stories, and Sir Oliver Lodge, a British physicist who played a key part in the development of radio.

Following his son's death in action in 1915, Sir Oliver laid out his beliefs and his evidence in a memoir, *Raymond, or Life and Death*, Methuen & Co 1916:

> Well, speaking for myself and with full and cautious responsibility, I have to state that as an outcome of my investigation into physical matters I have at length and quite gradually become convinced, after more than thirty years of study, not only that persistent individual existence is a fact, but that occasional communication across the chasm – with difficulty and under definite conditions – is possible.
>
> This is not a subject on which one comes lightly and easily to a conclusion, nor can the evidence be explained except to those who will give to it time and careful study; but clearly the conclusion is either folly and self-deception, or it is truth of the utmost importance to humanity –

Mrs Mary Evans saw it as truth.

Evans was born in Ramsgate, Kent on 12 August 1897. He attested in August 1915 in Canada where he and his widowed mother were then living. Evans served with the 75th Battalion Canadian Infantry and was killed in action on 30 September 1918 when the 75th led the dawn attack on the Cambrai-Douai railway cutting just south of Blécourt.

WHY THEN, GOD'S SOLDIER BE HE!

SECOND LIEUTENANT ARTHUR STANNUS JAGGER
ROYAL WELSH FUSILIERS
DIED 30 SEPTEMBER 1918
BURIED CHOCQUES MILITARY CEMETERY, FRANCE

Arthur Jagger was his parents' only child. His father, the former headmaster of Queen Elizabeth's Grammar School, Mansfield, signed for his inscription; it comes from *Macbeth Act 5 Scene 8*:

> ROSS: Your son, my lord, has paid a soldier's debt:
> ...
> SIWARD: Then he is dead?
> ROSS: Ay, and brought off the field: your cause of sorrow
> Must not be measured by his worth, for then
> It hath no end
> SIWARD: Had he his wounds before?
> ROSS: Ay, on the front.
> SIWARD: Why then, God's soldier be he!

Siward derived comfort from the fact that his son had died a soldier's death, facing the enemy, not with his back to it, not running away.

Jaggard left Malvern College in December 1916 for the Royal Military College, Sandhurst. Commissioned into the 9th Battalion Royal Welsh Fusiliers in December 1917, he joined them in France on 27 June 1918. The battalion were in action on 30 September:

> A & D companies under light barrage took part in an operation and successfully advanced line taking 10 prisoners and 1 machine gun. Our casualties were 3 officers wounded (of whom 1 died of wounds) 11 other ranks killed & 38 other ranks wounded.
> Battalion War Diary 9th Battalion Welsh Regiment 30 September 1918

Jagger, wounded in the head by shrapnel, died the same day.

RELIGION CHURCH OF IRELAND AN IRISHMAN LOYAL TO DEATH TO KING AND COUNTRY

PRIVATE WALTER McCLEAN MURRAY
ROYAL IRISH FUSILIERS
DIED 30 SEPTEMBER 1918 AGED 21
BURIED HOOGE CRATER CEMETERY, BELGIUM

Walter McClean Murray was a Protestant from Rockcorry, Co. Monaghan, the son of John Murray, the Rockcorry Petty Sessions Clerk, and his wife Mary Ann. Murray served with the 9th Battalion Royal Irish Fusiliers, one of the thirteen infantry battalions raised for the 36th Ulster Division. Many of the original members of the 9th had been raised from Armagh, Monaghan and Cavan Volunteers, units of the Ulster Volunteers, a unionist militia formed in 1912 to resist any attempts by the British Government to force Ireland to accept Home Rule. They did not want independence from England, they were 'loyal to death to King and Country', and if necessary they would fight that country to show their determination to remain part of it.

Murray went missing, presumed killed, on 30 September 1918 during the 9th Battalion's advance on the village of Moorseele, north east of the town of Menin. After initial success, the final advance was prevented by heavy machine gun fire from a string of fortified farms and pill boxes. Murray's body was discovered in April 1919 and eventually reburied in Hooge Crater Cemetery.

In 1920 the British Government passed the Government of Ireland Act, and in May 1921 Ireland was partitioned. The majority of Irish counties eventually formed the Irish Free State, but six of the nine counties of Ulster opted to remain part of the United Kingdom. Co. Monaghan opted to join the Irish Free State.

A Mr T. Murray of Broughshane Co. Antrim chose Walter Murray's inscription. Broughshane was eighty miles from Rockcorry and Antrim was one of the six counties that formed Northern Ireland and remained part of the United Kingdom. There is nothing to show how T. Murray was related to Walter Murray, but perhaps this fiercely Unionist family had migrated north of the border.

OH CANADA
HE STOOD ON GUARD FOR THEE

PRIVATE REGINALD GEORGE BOX
CANADIAN INFANTRY
DIED 1 OCTOBER 1918 AGED 24
SANCOURT BRITISH CEMETERY, FRANCE

Private Box's inscription comes from a patriotic Canadian song that has become Canada's national anthem and is the source of the Canadian Army's motto – *Vigilamus Pro Te*: we stand on guard for thee. It was neither of these things when Private Box's father, William Box, chose it.

Originally written in 1880, in French, the words were translated into English several times before Robert Stanley Weir's version, which he wrote in 1908, was settled on. In 1939 it became, de facto, Canada's national anthem, but was only officially adopted in 1980. Weir himself made various amendments to his original version and changes continue to be suggested and made. This is a version that Reginald Box would have recognised:

> O Canada!
> Our home and native land.
> True patriot love in all thy sons command.
> With glowing hearts we see thee rise,
> The True North strong and free!
> We stand on guard, O Canada,
> We stand on guard for thee.
> O Canada, Glorious and free.
> O Canada, we stand on guard for thee.
> O Canada, we stand on guard for thee!

Reginald Box was born in Cheltenham, Gloucestershire where his father was a jeweller and silversmith. In 1911, aged sixteen, he went to Canada and took up farming. He joined up in February 1916, served with the 16th Battalion Canadian Infantry and was killed on 1 October 1918 in the capture of the village of Sancourt during the battle for the Canal du Nord.

After the war, Reginald's older brother, Charles Henry Box, who had also served in the Canadian Infantry, returned to England to take over his father's jewellery business. In 1921, he and his wife named their first son Reginald after his brother.

BEHIND THE DARK CLOUD
IS A SILVER LINING

RIFLEMAN ERNEST FREDERICK WALDEN
LONDON REGIMENT (LONDON RIFLE BRIGADE)
DIED 1 OCTOBER 1918 AGED 19
BURIED CAMBRAI EAST MILITARY CEMETERY, FRANCE

It was John Milton (1608–1674) who first wrote about clouds and silver linings with the implication that even in the darkest night of trouble there can be a glimmer of hope.

> Was I deceived, or did a sable cloud
> Turn forth her silver lining on the night?
> *Comus* (1634)

By the end of the nineteenth century the saying had passed into popular usage. In Gilbert and Sullivan's *The Mikado* (1885) Yum-Yum's bridegroom tells her, 'Don't let's be downhearted! There's a silver lining to every cloud'. During the war, a set of Bamforth postcards showed a soldier dreamily smoking a cigarette with the words 'only gaze at the smoke clouds and never despair, for there's bound to be some silver lining somewhere'. However, it was the chorus from the popular patriotic song, *Keep the Home Fires Burning* (1914) by Ivor Novello (1893–1951), that gave the phrase its biggest boost:

> Keep the home fires burning,
> While your hearts are yearning.
> Though your lads are far away
> They dream of home.
> There's a silver lining
> Through the dark clouds shining,
> Turn the dark cloud inside out
> 'Til the boys come home.

Ernest Walden was the youngest of William and Mary Ann Walden's seven children. The family lived in Wansted, Essex. Ernest served in 'D' Company London Rifle Brigade, and was killed in the trenches on 1 October. On 30 September the battalion war diary reported that they had taken over extra frontage, held by C and D companies, at Palleul Lock. The next day the diary recorded: 'hostile artillery active over Palleul Lock during early morning & also at night; otherwise quiet day'.

BABY OF FAMILY
BORN GREEN BAY, WISC. U.S.A.
MOTHER STILL ANXIOUS
FOR HIS RETURN

PRIVATE ALBERT KICK
CANADIAN INFANTRY
DIED 1 OCTOBER 1918 AGED 29
BURIED SANCOURT BRITISH CEMETERY, FRANCE

Albert Kick was a Oneida First Nation American born on the Green Bay reservation in Wisconsin U.S.A. His family later moved to the reservation in Muncey, Ontario. His mother, Katherine Kick, chose his inscription, reflecting a Oneida concern for the afterlife of the dead person. It is possible that 'Mother still anxious for his return' meant that she still hoped her son was going to come home alive, but it is more likely that her concern was with his body because to traditional Oneida, the cycle of life is only complete when the dead person's spirit has returned to its place of origin. For this to happen it is important that the body should be among familiar people where specific burial customs, practices and rites can be performed to help the dead person's spirit back into the spirit world. If this does not happen it will be restless.

But, the British Army had banned the repatriation of soldiers' bodies. All Empire soldiers were to be buried in the countries where they died. The American military did allow repatriation but Albert Kick was a Canadian soldier in the British Army.

Kick and his brother, Ernest, briefly attended Carlisle Indian Industrial School, Pennsylvania. This Indian boarding school was founded on the principle that Native Americans, although the equal of European Americans, needed to be immersed in Euro-American culture in order to acquire the necessary skills to advance in life.

Albert Kick attested on 28 January 1916. He served with B Company, 4th Battalion Canadian Infantry, the same company as his brother Ernest, and was killed in action during the battle for the Canal du Nord. As reported in the battalion war diary:

> Battalion attacked Abancourt at Zero hour viz 0500 o'clock and fought forward with unsurpassed bravery under murderous Machine Gun and Artillery fire. Objectives not gained, but the Battalion did not have to give up one foot of ground they had won.

HIS BODY TO FAIR FRANCE
HIS PURE SOUL
UNTO HIS CAPTAIN CHRIST

SECOND LIEUTENANT BERNARD RICHARD PENDEREL-BRODHURST
ROYAL ENGINEERS
DIED 1 OCTOBER 1918 AGED 27
BURIED ST VAAST POST MILITARY CEMETERY, FRANCE

The name Bernard Richard Penderel-Brodhurst has a very particular ring to it, something that seems appropriate for the heir to the perpetual pension Charles II settled on his ancestor, Humphrey Penderel, for aiding his escape after the Battle of Worcester in 1651.

Penderel-Brodhurst, the only surviving son of James George Joseph Penderel-Brodhurst editor of *The Guardian*, was articled to a firm of architects when war broke out. An obituary in the *Architectural Review* outlined his war service. After enlisting in August 1914, he served in Britain as a PE instructor until July 1917. At this point he was commissioned into the Royal Engineers and went to France in April 1918.

On the evening of 1 October, Penderel-Brodhurst was shot at by a sniper as he emerged from a communication trench in an area of the front line not thought to have been particularly dangerous. The sniper missed. Penderel-Brodhurst turned to his companion and smiled but the next instant the sniper fired again and hit him. He died three hours later, three days before his 28th birthday and his first wedding anniversary.

Penderel-Brodhurst's inscription, which his father chose, comes from Shakespeare's *Richard II*. The words are spoken of Thomas Mowbray, Duke of Norfolk:

Many a time hath banish'd Norfolk fought
For Jesu Christ in glorious Christian field,
Streaming the ensign of the Christian cross
Against black pagans, Turks and Saracens;
And toil'd with works of war, retir'd himself
To Italy, and there, at Venice, gave
His body to that pleasant country's earth,
And his pure soul unto his captain Christ,
Under whose colours he had fought so long.

TERIBUS

MAJOR WILLIAM FRANCIS BEATTIE MC
ROYAL FIELD ARTILLERY
DIED 3 OCTOBER 1918 AGED 30
BURIED TINCOURT NEW BRITISH CEMETERY, FRANCE

By choosing this single Latin word, *Teribus*, William Francis Beattie's father elegantly linked several aspects of his son's life. The word is said to have been part of the battle cry of the men of Hawick at the Battle of Flodden in 1513 – 'Teribus ye Teri-Odin'. A nineteenth-century song tells how bands of English soldiers plundered the surrounding countryside in the months after the battle until the following year when a group of Hawick men attacked one of the bands and carried off its flag in what is known locally as the Battle of Hornshole. The history may be questionable but the legend remains very powerful and is still commemorated in Hawick.

In June 1914, the town marked the 400th anniversary of the 'battle' by erecting a bronze statue of a horseman holding the captured English banner. The sculptor, William Francis Beattie, had been born in Hawick, which made him a 'Teri', a Hawickman.

Beattie, a territorial soldier before the war, took a commission in the Royal Artillery and went to France in August 1915. Awarded a Military Cross in 1917 for rescuing some wounded soldiers under a heavy artillery barrage, he was badly gassed in April 1918 and spent five months recovering before returning to the front on 20 September. He died of wounds two weeks later.

The final touches were not made to Beattie's statue until 1921 when, in addition to an inscription commemorating the event, the following inscription was added:

> Merses Profundo Pulchrior Evenit
> Sculptor: Major William F. Beattie MC RFA
> A native of Hawick
> Born 1886 Killed in France 1918

The Latin is a quotation from Horace: Plunge it in the deep, it will emerge all the fairer. Thomas Beattie, William Beattie's father, carried out the work. William Francis Beattie was his parents' only child.

HIS LAST WORDS WERE
AS HE FELL
"GO ON 'C' COMPANY"

CAPTAIN WILLIAM McCARTHY BRAITHWAITE MC
AUSTRALIAN INFANTRY
DIED 3 OCTOBER 1918 AGED 25
BURIED PROSPECT HILL CEMETERY, GOUY, FRANCE

William Braithwaite was killed in action at Montbrehain, the Australian Infantry's last action on the Western Front. Three days later they were withdrawn for a period of rest. The war was over before they returned. Braithwaite, who served with the 22nd Battalion Australian Infantry, was killed charging a machine gun. The battalion's Report of Operations gives a brief glimpse of the action that day:

> There were several instances where determined resistance was offered by small groups of Machine Gunners [German], and an examination of the ground after the attack evidenced the fact that the bayonets had been used by our men to a greater extent than usual.

Braithwaite had worked with his father, whose tannery was the largest employer in Preston, Victoria. He enlisted in July 1916. A collection of his letters, held in the Australian National War Memorial, describe his active service – Bapaume, Bullecourt, Ypres, Broodseinde, Villers-Bretonneaux, Amiens – and comment on the futility of war. He was awarded the Military Cross,

> For conspicuous gallantry in leading his men into the enemy's trenches during the attack near Bullecourt on 3 May 1917. Although twice wounded he persevered with the work of consolidating the position and leading bombing parties against the enemy strongpoints.

Wounded in the arm and face that same day, Braithwaite was back in action by July. He was wounded again at Franvillers in June 1918, had two weeks leave in England in September and was killed in action soon after his return.

His father, also William Braithwaite, chose his inscription. Although he and his wife had six daughters, William was their only son. William Braithwaite, senior, died on 5 August 1922 on a visit to Europe with his wife to see their son's grave.

I SAW THE POWERS OF DARKNESS
PUT TO FLIGHT
I SAW THE MORNING BREAK

LIEUTENANT BRUCE GARIE THOMSON
AUSTRALIAN FLYING CORPS
DIED 3 OCTOBER 1918 AGED 24
BURIED PROSPECT HILL CEMETERY, GOUY, FRANCE

These lines come from a poem called *Between Midnight and Morning*, said to have been found on the body of an Australian soldier killed at Gallipoli, with the implication that the soldier wrote it. A copy of the poem could easily have been found on the body of an Australian soldier but he most definitely did not write it because it was written by Owen Seaman (1861–1936), the editor of *Punch*, and published in *King Albert's Book* in December 1914.

> You that have faith to look with fearless eyes
> Beyond the tragedy of a world at strife,
> And trust that out of night and death shall rise
> The dawn of ampler life:
>
> Rejoice, whatever anguish rend your heart,
> That God has given you, for a priceless dower,
> To live in these great times and have your part
> In Freedom's crowning hour.
>
> That you may tell your sons who see the light
> High in the heavens, their heritage to take: –
> "I saw the powers of darkness put to flight!
> I saw the morning break!"

Thomson, born and raised in Kapunda, South Australia, enlisted in November 1914. He served initially with the 3rd Field Ambulance before qualifying as an observer and joining No. 3 Squadron AFC on reconnaissance, bombing and artillery spotting duties.

At 6 am on the morning of the 3 October 1918, Thomson and his pilot Gould-Taylor took off from the airfield at Bouvincourt and never returned. Their crashed machine was found three days later. Beside it were two graves

NOT SINCE HER BIRTH
HAS OUR EARTH SEEN
SUCH WORTH LOOSED UPON IT

LANCE SERGEANT ALEXANDER LORIMER RIDDELL
CANADIAN INFANTRY
DIED 3 OCTOBER 1918 AGED 33
BURIED DUISANS BRITISH CEMETERY, ETRUN, FRANCE

Alexander Lorimer Riddell, army service number 706968, son of George and Margaret Riddell of Rosehearty, Fraserburgh, Aberdeenshire, was born in Scotland in 1885. In 1906, aged twenty-one, he went to Canada and settled in Nanamo, British Columbia. He enlisted in the Canadian Infantry in February 1916, sailed from Halifax in July and joined his unit in the field in February 1917. Wounded at Vimy Ridge in April 1917, he returned to Rosehearty in December and he married Jean Arthur. After two weeks leave he returned to the front and died of wounds received in action on 3 October 1918.

This information comes from Riddell's family for his entry in the *Marquis du Ruvigny's Roll of Honour*. So why on his Canadian attestation form did Riddell say that he was born in New South Wales, Australia? And why did he give as his next of kin a step-father, Donald Riddell of Lincoln, Nebraska, when he did not have a step-father?

His wife chose his inscription from verse three of Rudyard Kipling's poem *The Children*, a savage indictment of a society that led its innocent children into war:

> They bought us anew with their blood, forbearing to blame us,
> Those hours which we had not made good when the judgement o'ercame us.
> They believed us and perished for it. Our statecraft, our learning
> Delivered them bound to the pit and alive to the burning
> Whither they mirthfully hastened as jostling for honour –
> Not since her birth has our earth seen such worth loosed upon her.

Never before has our earth seen such wonderful people thrown away and wasted in this manner. But, as Kipling acknowledged, we can rail all we like against what has happened, we can regret it, we can try to make amends, but in the end what is the point because, as the last line of the poem asks, 'Who shall return us our children?' And the answer, of course, is no one.

THIS EARTH HATH BORNE
NO SIMPLER, NOBLER MAN

LIEUTENANT-COLONEL EDWARD HILLS NICHOLSON DSO & BAR
ROYAL FUSILIERS
DIED 4 OCTOBER 1918 AGED 38
BURIED UNICORN CEMETERY, VENDHUILE, FRANCE

Ethel Nicholson chose her husband's inscription from the epitaph Tennyson wrote for his friend General Gordon, killed in the Sudan in January 1885:

> Warrior of God, man's friend, and tyrant's foe
> Now somewhere dead far in the waste Soudan,
> Thou livest in all hearts, for all men know
> This earth has never born a simpler, nobler man.

It is difficult to overestimate Gordon's fame; he was one of the Victorian era's biggest military heroes, his achievements summarised on his memorial in St Paul's Cathedral:

> He saved an Empire by his warlike genius, he ruled vast provinces with justice, wisdom, and power. And lastly obedient to his sovereign's command, he died in the heroic attempt to save men, women and children from imminent and deadly peril.

Tennyson's epitaph, originally published in a letter to *The Times* on 7 May 1885, does not feature on any of Gordon's public monuments, but in the Gordon Boys' National Memorial Home, Woking, one of a series of boys' homes established throughout the country in his memory.

Edward Nicholson was a professional soldier who joined the army on leaving school in 1900. He served in South Africa and India and at the time of his death was commanding the 3rd Battalion Royal Fusiliers. He was killed on 4 October 1918 in an attack on a German stronghold at Richmond Copse.

Nicholson was one of seven children: four sons and three daughters. All four sons served in the war: Bruce Nicholson was killed on 3 May 1917 and Victor Nicholson two months later on 9 August. Walter Nicholson survived the war but died whilst serving with the RAF in 1943.

SEE THAT MY GRAVE IS GREEN

PRIVATE WILFRED LEWIS SIMMONS
CANADIAN ARMY SERVICE CORPS
DIED 4 OCTOBER 1918 AGED 23
BURIED ST SEVER CEMETERY EXTENSION, FRANCE

See That My Grave is Kept Green is a sentimental American song written by Gus Williams in 1876. A blues version by Blind Lemon Jackson (1893–1929) based on Williams' original song but with the final word of the line changed to 'clean' not 'green' is world famous among jazz aficionados. The words, 'See that my grave is kept clean' appear on Jackson's grave.

In Williams' song, the singer asks that when he is dead his grave will be kept green:

> When from the world and its hopes I go,
> Leaving for ever the scene
> Though others are dear, ah, will you then
> See that my grave's kept green.

Although others are dear, don't forget me – and try to think of the happy times.

> Tell me you'll think of the happy past
> Think of the joys we have seen.
> This one little promise keep for me
> See that my grave's kept green.

Wilfred Simmons was a student at the Hamilton Normal School when he enlisted in March 1916. He served originally with the 120th Battalion before transferring to the military transport section of the Canadian Forestry Corps. This was, in effect, a military lumberjack unit, cutting down forests in England, Scotland and France to meet the army's insatiable demand for timber.

In August 1918 he became ill with appendicitis. On the 24th, he was admitted to hospital and operated on. His condition seemed to improve but later his condition worsened and he died two months later of what was described as 'recurrent appendicitis'. His father chose his inscription.

RECTE FACIENDO SECURUS

LIEUTENANT ROBERT INGLIS MC
BLACK WATCH
DIED 5 OCTOBER 1918 AGED 39
BURIED DOINGT COMMUNAL CEMETERY EXTENSION, PÉRONNE, FRANCE

Recte faciendo securus – by acting justly you need fear nothing – is the Inglis family motto.

Robert and Isabella Inglis of Lovestone, Girvan, Ayrshire had ten children: four daughters and five sons. You might be able to tell where this is going. The eldest son, Alexander, was killed in South Africa in 1901, the youngest son, David, was killed in France on 19 December 1914, Charles, the third son, on 25 September 1915, and Robert, the second eldest, died of wounds on 5 October 1918. Only one son, William, survived.

Prior to the war, Robert Inglis had been a sergeant in the Scottish Horse Yeomanry and joint factor with his father on the Bargany Estate in Ayrshire. Mobilized on the outbreak of war, he was commissioned Second Lieutenant in September 1914 and after a period of service in England embarked on 1 January 1916 to join the Egyptian Expeditionary Force on the Suez Canal. In October 1916 the Scottish Yeomanry became the 13th Battalion Royal Highlanders (Black Watch) and in June 1918 the battalion moved to France.

Inglis was wounded on 3 October 1918 when 'C' Company co-operated with the Royal Dublin Fusiliers in an attack on Le Catelet and Gouy. The battalion war diary mentions that, 'there was considerable sniping causing several casualties': one officer and thirteen other ranks killed, one officer and twenty-four other ranks wounded. Inglis died the next day.

Recte faciendo securus – by acting justly you need fear nothing. The reference is to salvation rather than to having nothing to fear in this earthly life.

SUNKEN ROAD CEMETERY

TILL GABRIEL
SOUNDS THE LAST RALLY

PRIVATE JAMES BELL HARVEY MM
ROYAL ARMY MEDICAL CORPS
DIED 9 OCTOBER 1918 AGED 21
BURIED SUNKEN ROAD CEMETERY, BOISLEUX-ST MARC, FRANCE

It is the Archangel Gabriel who will sound the last rally – the trumpet call heralding the arrival of the Day of Judgement. Rally is a military word for a trumpet or bugle call that is sounded to recall the cavalry after a charge – to bring them home. Gabriel also calls people home, home to their father in heaven.

Harvey's inscription is taken from the last line of *The Trumpeter*, a song originally written in 1904 by J. Francis Barron, which became very popular during the First World War, especially after 1915 when it was recorded by John McCormack. In verse one the trumpeter sounds reveille to rouse the sleeping soldiers from their tents. In verse two he sounds the charge, and in verse three the rally. But for all its popularity and stirring military associations, the song makes no concessions to the fact that war is terrible, as the often-omitted last line of verse two declares: '"And it's Hell!" said the Trumpeter tall'.

James Harvey, the son of a Glasgow tram conductor, served with the 1st/2nd Lowland Field Ambulance, Royal Army Medical Corps and died of wounds in a Casualty Clearing Station in Boisleux-St Marc on 9 October 1918. His inscription comes from the last line of the song:

> Trumpeter, what are you sounding now!
> (Is it the call I'm seeking!)
> 'Lucky for you if you hear it all,
> For my trumpet's but faintly speakin'.
> I'm callin' 'em home – come home! come home!
> Tread light o'er the dead in the valley.
> Who are lyin' around face down to the ground,
> And they can't hear me sound the 'Rally'.
> But they'll hear it again in a grand refrain,
> When Gabriel sounds the last 'Rally'.

HE SLEEPS
WITH THE UNRETURNING BRAVE

SECOND LIEUTENANT HUGH PRICE
WEST YORKSHIRE REGIMENT
DIED 11 OCTOBER 1918 AGED 27
BURIED ST AUBERT BRITISH CEMETERY, FRANCE

Hugh Price was killed in action on 11 October 1918 when the 49th Division took the village of St Aubert where he is buried. The battalion war diary described the day:

> Zero hour 9 am. An advance of 1,000 yards was made the Bn. passing through the Canadians who were holding the line. Towards noon the enemy counter-attacked with tanks & we withdrew 500 yds to Sunken Road ... where enemy were held for the night. During the night 11th-12th the enemy withdrew ...

On the 12 October the German Government followed up their note of 3 October with a second note to President Woodrow Wilson expressing their willingness to negotiate an armistice. The war had a month to run.

'The unreturning brave' is an old euphemism for the war dead. In *Childe Harold's Pilgrimage* (1818) Byron, writing about the dead of Waterloo, describes how:

> ... Ardennes waves above them her green leaves,
> Dewy with Nature' tear drops, as they pass
> Grieving, if aught inanimate e're grieves
> Over the unreturning brave, – alas!

John W Forney used the term for the American Civil War dead in his poem, The Men Who Fell at Baltimore 1861.

> As over every honoured grave
> Where sleeps the 'Unreturning Brave,'
> A mother sobs, a young wife moans,
> A father for a lost one groans ...

And Mrs Catherine Price, quite possibly unaware of Forney's poem, echoes his words on the grave of her eldest son.

MAKE HIM TO BE NUMBERED WITH THY SAINTS O LORD IN GLORY EVERLASTING

BRIGADIER GENERAL STUART CAMPBELL TAYLOR DSO
GENERAL STAFF
DIED 11 OCTOBER 1918 AGED 45
BURIED LA KREULE MILITARY CEMETERY, HAZEBROUCK, FRANCE

Stuart Campbell Taylor, a career soldier, was one of seventy-eight generals to die as a result of enemy action in the First World War. Commissioned into the King's Own Yorkshire Light Infantry in 1892, he served in Tirah on the North West Frontier, Mauritius, South Africa, Crete and Northern Nigeria before retiring from the Army in 1911 at the age of thirty-nine.

Taylor re-joined his regiment on the outbreak of war, taking command of the 11th Battalion. In May 1915 he was promoted to command the 15th West Yorkshire Regiment, the Leeds Pals, where his men described him as 'a martinet but very fair'.

Wounded in May 1916 he was therefore not with his men when they attacked towards the village of Serre at 7.30 on the morning of 1 July 1916, losing 15 officers and 233 men killed in the opening minutes of the Somme offensive. In May 1917, whilst still in command of the regiment, he was awarded the DSO for conspicuous gallantry and in March 1918 was promoted Brigadier-General in command of 93rd Brigade, 31st Division.

On the morning of 1 October, Taylor was on a tour of inspection of the front line when fatally injured by shrapnel from a bursting shell. He died ten days later in a Casualty Clearing Station at La Kreule. He is buried in the cemetery there between a rifleman and a private, exemplifying the War Grave Commission's insistence on the equality in death of all soldiers regardless of rank or social position – a sentiment of which Taylor would have approved.

Stuart Campbell Taylor was educated at the Dragon School in Oxford, while his father, Dr James Campbell Taylor (1833–1900), was the organist at New College, and at Bedford Grammar School. His mother chose his inscription from the *Te Deum*:

> We therefore pray thee, help Thy servants: whom thou hast redeemed
> with Thy precious blood,
> Make them to be numbered with Thy saints: in glory everlasting.

HE SLEEPS
THE SOUL, FROM EARTH'S CONTROL
RELEASED
SEES HEAVEN'S LIGHT

PRIVATE JAMES EDWARD ALLEN
DUKE OF WELLINGTON'S WEST RIDING REGIMENT
DIED 11 OCTOBER 1918 AGED 20
BURIED WELLINGTON CEMETERY, RIEUX-EN-CAMBRÉSIS, FRANCE

Private Allen was born and brought up in Walsall, Staffordshire where his father was a policeman. His inscription comes from *The Glorious Dead*, a poem written by Joseph Turner and published in *Songs from the Heart of England*, an anthology of Walsall poetry edited by Alfred Moss and published by T. Fisher Unwin in 1920.

James Allen attested on 5 August 1916, one month short of his eighteenth birthday. He went to France in October 1917, one month after his nineteenth. He served with the 4th Battalion Duke of Wellington's West Riding Regiment and was killed one month before the end of the war in an attack on the village of Rieux-en-Cambrésis. The battalion went 'over the top' at 09.00 hours. All appeared to be going well until 10.30,

> when the enemy suddenly counter-attacked heavily on both flanks with Tanks and infantry. The Tanks, which were German not captured British & about 8 in number, had been lying out of sight in the low ground ...

Herbert Allen chose his son's inscription. According to Turner's poem:

> They do not die
> Who fall
> At freedom's call
> In battle for the right.
> ...
> They do but sleep:
> The soul,
> From earth's control
> Released sees Heaven's light

AND AFTER THE SUNSET
IN THE UNKNOWN NIGHT
JOY CANNOT CEASE
D.G.C. 5.4.16

PRIVATE DAVID GEOFFREY COLLINS
GRENADIER GUARDS
DIED 11 OCTOBER 1918 AGED 19
BURIED DELSAUX FARM CEMETERY, BEUGNY, FRANCE

The initials at the bottom of the inscription belong to the casualty, David Geoffrey Collins, who his father described in the War Graves Commission register as a 'poet, botanist, mathematician and peace lover'. This would suggest that Collins wrote the lines his father used – on 5 April 1916.

Collins had an unusual upbringing. His father, Edwin Hyman Simeon Henry Collins, was an erudite man with an original mind. Known as a radical educational thinker, he believed fervently that children should not begin formal education before they were nine; that they should never be taught to read but should learn themselves when they were ready, and that all their lessons should be held outside at all times.

Edwin Collins brought his children up according to his beliefs, refusing to let them go to school, which caused him to be prosecuted for child neglect. But he used the witness box to gain publicity, claiming that his methods would make his children 'more useful, more independent, more robust in character, better in physique and with greater powers of assimilating knowledge' than other children.

David Collins was called up when he was eighteen and sent to France in August 1918, just after his nineteenth birthday. He served with the 1st Battalion Grenadier Guards and died three months later of wounds received that day in the capture of a German strongpoint at Delsaux Farm.

David Collins' headstone is inscribed with the Star of David. His father, who described himself on the War Graves Commission form as the Rev. Edwin Collins, was born a Jew, trained and practised as a rabbi, and preached for some time as a Christian Unitarian minister before returning fully to the Jewish faith. Edwin Collins chose his son's inscription, using his son's words to express his own belief that death is not the end.

WE FALL TO RISE
ARE BAFFLED TO FIGHT BETTER
SLEEP TO WAKE

CAPTAIN WILLIAM BOYD JACK MC
ROYAL ARMY MEDICAL CORPS
DIED 11 OCTOBER 1918 AGED 38
BURIED FRESNOY-LE-GRAND COMMUNAL CEMETERY EXTENSION, FRANCE

Captain Jack, Medical Officer for the 5th Battalion Leicestershire Regiment, was killed during a German counter-attack at Fresnoy. He had gone to the aid of a badly wounded stretcher-bearer and was badly wounded himself. He died that evening.

When the 5th Battalion's regimental history was published in 1919, Jack was described as 'the invaluable WB Jack', 'as usual wonderfully calm', and of his death it said:

> Captain Jack had been with us just a year, and we felt very keenly the loss of his cheerful presence at Battalion HQ, for he was one of those men who were never depressed, and even in the worst of times used to keep us happy.

William Boyd Jack, born and educated in Scotland, a married man with three children, was practicing medicine in Kendal, Westmorland when the war broke out. He joined up in March 1917. His Military Cross was awarded for 'conspicuous gallantry and devotion to duty' when on 24 September 1918 he worked in the open, under constant gas and HE shell fire, from 5 am until 3 am the following morning, 'his fine conduct saved many lives'.

Mrs Jean Jack, his wife, chose his inscription from *Epilogue*, Robert Browning's final poem in his final volume of poetry, *Asolando*, which was published on the day he died:

> One who never turned his back but marched breast forward,
> Never doubted clouds would break,
> Never dreamed, though right were worsted, wrong would triumph,
> Held we fall to rise, are baffled to fight better,
> Sleep to wake.

It is thought that Browning summarised his own attitude to life in this verse: how adversity never defeated him, how whatever happened was for the right, and how at the end of our lives we would awake to a new life in heaven.

IN FOREIGN SOIL SHE LAYS
AND IN THAT EARTH
A RICHER DUST CONCEALS

NURSING SISTER SOPHIA HILLING ARRC
QUEEN ALEXANDRA'S IMPERIAL MILITARY NURSING SERVICE
DIED 12 OCTOBER 1918 AGED 34
BURIED TOURGEVILLE MILITARY CEMETERY, FRANCE

These are not exactly the words Rupert Brooke wrote but when Mrs Sarah Hilling chose her daughter's inscription she had Brooke's poem, *The Soldier*, firmly in her mind:

> If I should die, think only this of me;
> That there's some corner of a foreign field
> That is for ever England. There shall be
> In that rich earth a richer dust concealed;
> A dust whom England bore, shaped, made aware,
> Gave, once, her flowers to love, her ways to roam ...

Sophia Hilling was born in Deptford, South London. Her father, Samuel Hilling, was a rag cutter and her mother a charwoman. In 1911, Sophia was a sick nurse working at the Birmingham Workhouse Infirmary. On the outbreak of war, she joined Queen Alexandra's Imperial Military Nursing Service Reserve (QAIMNSR), one of more than 10,000 trained nurses who did so during the war years. Prior to 1914, nurses had to be of impeccable social standing but the demand for them removed that barrier. During the war you only had to have had three years approved training, be over twenty-five ... and unmarried.

Hilling held the Royal Red Cross Medal (Second Class), awarded to nurses for 'special exertions in providing for the nursing of sick and wounded soldiers and sailors'. At the time of the award, March 1917, she was working at the Welsh Metropolitan War Hospital in Whitchurch near Cardiff, which at that time was treating both orthopaedic and psychiatric patients.

By 1918 Hilling was the Home Sister at No. 72 General Hospital, Trouville. On 12 October, E Maud McCarthy, Matron-in-Chief of the BEF in France and Flanders, recorded in her official diary that she had wired the Matron-in-Chief at the War Office to report to the Director General of Medical Services that Sister S. Hilling, was on the 'Dangerously ill' list with pneumonia; the next day McCarthy wired to say Hilling had died.

HE JOINED THE FORCES
AT 15½ YEARS
AND DID HIS DUTY
TILL DEATH

RIFLEMAN ALBERT KNOWLES
KING'S ROYAL RIFLE CORPS
DIED 12 OCTOBER 1918 AGED 19
BURIED AMERVAL COMMUNAL CEMETERY EXTENSION, SOLESMES, FRANCE

Born in January 1899, Albert Knowles was therefore fifteen and a half when war broke out in August 1914. Although far too young, he volunteered immediately. You were meant to be eighteen before you could enlist, and nineteen before you could serve abroad but in the early days of the war, if you said you were nineteen, and looked nineteen, the army took your word for it. Much is made of recruiting sergeants wilfully turning a blind eye to obviously underage boys but in fact the army did not want weaklings: you needed to be able to march long distances, carrying your own kit, you needed to be strong.

Knowles obviously managed to convince the authorities. His medal card shows that he went to France in September 1915. At this point he was just over sixteen and a half. By the time he reached the legal age for serving at the front in January 1918 he had been there for three years.

Knowles was killed as the 16th Battalion King's Royal Rifle Corps tried to cross the River Selle. For all that the end of the war was only a month away, for all that the Germans were already putting out peace feelers, their soldiers were still fiercely resisting Allied attacks so that by noon on the 12th the 16th Battalion, which had been charged with taking the line of the Le Cateau-Solesmes railway and the surrounding high ground, had been forced to withdraw, 'disorganised', with very high casualties.

Albert Knowles may have deceived the army authorities about his age but his mother put that right on his headstone. There's a sense of pride in her choice of words, not so much pride in her deception but in the fact that even though he was only fifteen he had wanted to do his duty, and that he continued to do it 'till death'.

Albert was one of James and Martha Knowles' four sons. His eldest brother, Ernest, who served with the 3rd Battalion Grenadier Guards, died of wounds at a Casualty Clearing Station at Gezaincourt on 30 April 1918.

NO KING OR SAINT
HAD TOMB SO PROUD
AS HE WHOSE FLAG
BECOMES HIS SHROUD

SAPPER JAMES JOSEPH LEONARD
ROYAL ENGINEERS
DIED 13 OCTOBER 1918 AGED 30
BURIED CAMBRIN MILITARY CEMETERY, FRANCE

This inscription comes from *Nationality* by Thomas Osborne Davis (1814–1845). Verse one declares that a nation's voice is a solemn thing and should be respected; verse two that a nation's flag, unfurled in the cause of Liberty, should be guarded 'till Death or Victory', with the assurance that anyone who dies defending it, 'whose flag becomes his shroud', will have an honoured grave. Verse three insists that God gave nations the right to defend themselves with the sword against a foreign yoke.

So far, so patriotic, until you realise that the nation entitled to its voice, entitled to just and equal laws, is Ireland, and that to Davis the foreign yoke belonged to England.

The Leonards were a Roman Catholic family from Brackaville, a rural community near Coalisland Co. Tyrone. Sapper Leonard's mother chose his inscription. It is not possible to know what the family's politics were. Thomas Osborne Davis, the author of the poem was a Protestant who believed Irish nationalism was based on culture, language and Catholic Emancipation, not republicanism. Co. Tyrone did not join the Irish Free State in 1921. It remained part of the United Kingdom as one of the six counties of Northern Ireland, but Coalisland in particular was not without its share of 'troubles' in the late 20th Century.

James 'Joe' Leonard was a volunteer; his medal card shows that he arrived in France on 29 September 1915. He served throughout the war with the 157th Field Company Royal Engineers. In October 1918 the Company were based in Auchy constructing pontoons for the crossing of the Heutedeule Canal and attempting to stop a leak in the canal bank. The diary for 13 October:

> No. 3 [Section] in canal cut. Sprs Leonard and Dunnington killed and
> the stopping of the leak was not successful.

HE WAS A PRISONER
DEATH SET HIM FREE

PRIVATE JAMES GILES CROSS
LINCOLNSHIRE REGIMENT
DIED 13 OCTOBER 1918 AGED 32
BURIED HAUTMONT COMMUNAL CEMETERY, FRANCE

Private Cross's wife meant her husband's inscription both literally and metaphorically; James Cross was a prisoner, a prisoner of war, and death did set him free. Usually when inscriptions talk about the freedom of death they mean that the dead person has been set free from the bonds of this world, as in this often quoted passage from Shelley's *Adonais*:

> He has outsoared the shadow of our night;
> Envy and calumny and hate and pain,
> And that unrest which men miscall delight,
> Can touch him not and torture not again

Cross died of pneumonia in a German hospital in Hautmont. The town had been in German hands since the earliest days of the war and was not captured by the British until 8 November. James Cross had been in German hands since 16 April 1918.

He served with the 1st Battalion Lincolnshire Regiment, which went into the front line on 12 April in the Wytschaete Sector. At 4.30 am on the morning of the 16th the Germans subjected the line to a heavy and continuous bombardment before attacking at 5.45 am under cover of dense fog. They broke through the British lines. However, according to a report Brigadier General G.H. Gater compiled for his superiors, the Lincolns stood firm:

> and fought it out to the last. No officer, platoon or individual surrendered and the fighting was prolonged until 6.30 am. ... The withdrawal was covered by the Adjutant, Captain McKellar, with revolver and bombs, firing into the enemy at close quarters.

After the engagement, James Cross was among the missing. Eventually Mrs Cross learnt through the Red Cross that he had been taken prisoner, and was now dead. Cross's younger brother, Albert, was killed in action on 22 March 1918 and is commemorated on the Pozières Memorial.

THIS GRAVE WAS VISITED
BY HIS PARENTS
SUNDAY SEPT. 30TH 1923
R.I.P.

CORPORAL THOMAS MCBRIDE
EAST LANCASHIRE REGIMENT
DIED 13 OCTOBER 1918 AGED 23
BURIED ORCHARD DUMP CEMETERY, ARLEUX-EN-GOHELLE, FRANCE

If Thomas McBride's headstone inscription says that his parents visited his grave in September 1923 it means that his permanent headstone had not yet been erected. If it had been it would have been too late to have this inscription carved on it. This means that five years after McBride's death his grave was still only marked by a temporary wooden cross. It is a good illustration of the size of the War Graves Commission's task and of the length of time it took to construct the war cemeteries.

Thomas McBride, at the time of the 1911 census a scavenger in a cotton mill, someone who cleaned up the cotton fluff that accumulated under the machinery, was a volunteer who first saw active service on 25 September 1915. (His medal card says 1914 but as he is entitled to the 1915 Star not the 1914 Star this must be a mistake). He was killed on 13 October, the day after the 2nd Battalion East Lancashire Regiment took Douai prison, 'capturing two prisoners and killing some in the operation' (War Diary 25th Brigade).

It is likely that McBride's parents made their visit to his grave under the auspices of one of the charitable organisations that arranged tours for the bereaved. These were usually called 'pilgrimages' to differentiate them from battlefield visits made by the merely curious. Travel on the continent was expensive, complicated and for most people rare. A St Barnabas Society tour cost in the region of £4, a lot of money when £3 was the average weekly wage for the majority of men in the 1920s. And the situation was made even more difficult by the fact that few workers who earned less than £250 a year were entitled to holiday anyway. If you did not use an organisation like St Barnabas the visit was likely to cost £20.

Strictly speaking, Thomas McBride's parents, John and Ellen McBride, did not visit his grave in 1923. Ellen McBride died in 1900, at or just after the birth of Thomas's younger sister, Winifrid. It was his father and his stepmother, Mary Jane, who came.

WHAT CRUEL FOLLY IS WAR!
IT ROBS US OF OUR DEAREST

PRIVATE LAURANCE HERBERT HEBDITCH
LONDON REGIMENT
DIED 14 OCTOBER 1918 AGED 21
BURIED AUBERS RIDGE BRITISH CEMETERY, AUBERS, FRANCE

Mr William Hebditch of Selborne, Church Street, Martock, has received the sad intelligence that his eldest son, Private Laurance H. Hebditch, Divisional Observer, attached to the Headquarters, 47th Division, was killed in action on the evening of the 15th inst. Deceased, who was 21 years of age, was formerly on the staff of Parrs Bank at Tiverton. He enlisted at 18 and had been in France for nearly 2½ years. A letter has been received by Mr Hebditch from one of the officers, in which he says: – "I am very sorry to tell you that your son was killed in action on the 15th instant. I cannot tell you how sorry I am to lose him, as, apart from being a good observer, he was a very quiet, good natured boy, and such a good fellow. We buried him, and the section put a cross to mark his grave."
Western Chronicle 1 November 1918

Hebditch's father chose his inscription, insisting that the Commission made sure to engrave an exclamation mark, to indicate strong emotion, at the end of the first line.

This inscription is further evidence that the War Graves Commission was happy to allow inscriptions that criticised war in general, this war in particular, and even those that questioned the cause for which men died. After all, in this case, Mr Hebditch was doing no more than echoing the sentiments of General William Tecumseh Sherman the Union general who in 1860 warned the American South of the danger of provoking war should they secede from the Union:

> It is all folly, madness, a crime against civilization! You speak so lightly of war; you don't know what you're talking about. War is a terrible thing!

And later, on 12 September 1864, Sherman wrote to the Mayor of Atlanta, just before he burned the city to the ground:

> War is cruelty, and you cannot refine it; and those who brought war into our country deserve all the curses and maledictions a people can pour out.

AUBERS RIDGE
BRITISH CEMETERY

LIFE IS VERY SWEET BROTHER WHO WOULD WISH TO DIE

RIFLEMAN GERALD OSCAR SMITH
ROYAL IRISH RIFLES
DIED 14 OCTOBER 1918 AGED 25
BURIED TYNE COT CEMETERY, BELGIUM

'Life is sweet brother.'

'Do you think so?'

'Think so! – There's night and day, brother, both sweet things; sun, moon and stars, brother, all sweet things; there's likewise a wind on the heath. Life is very sweet, brother; who would wish to die?'

Lavengro 1851

George Borrow (1803–1881)

This partly autobiographical novel received a very cool reception when it was first published. Sales picked up after Borrow's death, encouraged by the opinion of critics like Theodore Watts who wrote in the introduction to the 1893 edition: 'There are passages in *Lavengro* which are unsurpassed in the prose literature of England'. Smith's inscription could be said to come from one such passage.

A corn dealer in civilian life, as was his father, Smith served with the 15th Battalion Royal Irish Rifles and was missing, believed killed in action, on the morning of 14 October in the battalion's attack on Moorseele. His body was not discovered until January 1921 when the fact that it still had its identity disc meant that Smith could be buried in a marked grave.

Gerald Smith was a married man with at least two children, sons Roy and Phillip. Phillip, a twenty-two-year-old sergeant serving with 10 Squadron, RAF Bomber Command, was killed in action on 6 November 1940, and twenty-nine-year-old Roy, a constable serving with the Palestine Police Force, was killed in a bomb explosion on 20 October 1946.

BOYHOOD'S
SCARCE CONSCIOUS BREATH
CHEERFULLY GIVEN
LEST WE FORGET

SERJEANT LOWRY LEES
LONDON REGIMENT (LONDON SCOTTISH)
DIED 14 OCTOBER 1918 AGED 22
BURIED DERRY HOUSE CEMETERY NO. 2, WIJTSCHATE, BELGIUM

Serjeant Lees' inscription combines a line from Rudyard Kipling's *Recessional*, with some from an extremely obscure poem, *Tombe des Anglais*, written by an equally obscure poet, Hagar Paul. Paul's poem references the Guards Grave in the Forêt de Retz where the 4th Guards Brigade fought a fierce rearguard action on 1 September 1914. The inscription comes from the last verse:

> Boyhood's scarce conscious breath
> Cheerfully given –
> None to record each death,
> How each had striven –
> Greater love no man hath
> This side of Heaven.

The Guardsmen were killed in the second month of the war, Lowry Lees was killed in the penultimate month when the 2nd/14th's attack on Quest Farm was met with 'a considerable amount of MG fire and warm resistance from defended pill boxes'.

The line from Recessional – Lest we forget – has become associated with military remembrance, 'lest we forget' the sacrifice of our soldiers. But that was not what Kipling meant. Written in 1897, at the end of the celebrations to mark Queen Victoria's Diamond Jubilee, Kipling was warning against triumphalism: all Empires are transient and in our pride of the moment we must never forget the human values we should have learnt from God.

> Lo, all our pomp of yesterday
> Is one with Nineveh and Tyre!
> Judge of the Nations, spare us yet,
> Lest we forget – lest we forget.

WITH THE VISION SPLENDID
HE SHALL SMILE BACK
AND NEVER KNOW REGRET

SECOND LIEUTENANT ANDREW RUSSELL BENNET
ROYAL AIR FORCE
DIED 14 OCTOBER 1918 AGED 22
BURIED DADIZEELE NEW BRITISH CEMETERY, BELGIUM

> Here – or hereafter – you shall see it ended,
> This mighty work to which your souls are set;
> If from beyond – then, with the vision splendid,
> You shall smile back and never know regret.

John Oxenham (the pseudonym for the popular and prolific poet William Arthur Dunkerley, 1852–1941) originally wrote this verse for his poem *Christs All! Our Boys Who Have Gone to the Front*. Later, Oxenham repeated the same verse in another poem, *The Vision Splendid*, published in a collection of poetry of the same name. And what is the 'vision splendid'? It is the time envisaged in the *Book of Revelation* 7:9-10 and perhaps best represented in the first verse of Doris N. Rendell's Salvation Army hymn:

> We have caught the vision splendid
> Of a world which is to be,
> When the pardoning love of Jesus
> Freely flows from sea to sea,
> When all men from strife and anger,
> Greed and selfishness are free,
> When nations live together
> In sweet peace and harmony.

Observer Andrew Bennet served with 82 Squadron on artillery spotting and photo reconnaissance duties. He and his pilot, Captain Humphrey Flowers, were shot down over Ledeghem, some sources say in aerial combat, others by ground fire as no German fighter claimed a corresponding kill that day. Twelve days later, his nineteen-year-old brother, Alexander, a private in the Durham Light Infantry, died of wounds received in action that day. Their widowed mother, Mrs Agnes Bennet, chose both their inscriptions. Alexander's reads: 'Until the day breaks and the shadows flee away'.

SON OF
SIR GEORGE WHITEHEAD
AND LADY WHITEHEAD
DEUS VULT

LIEUTENANT GEORGE WILLIAM EDENDALE WHITEHEAD
ROYAL AIR FORCE
DIED 17 OCTOBER 1918 AGED 23
BURIED HARLEBEKE NEW BRITISH CEMETERY, BELGIUM

George Whitehead and his observer, Reginald Griffiths, were artillery spotting over Lauwe when they were shot down at 7.50 am on the morning of 17 October 1917. The town was still in German hands and the two airmen were buried together by the Germans in a communal grave. It was five years before their bodies were exhumed and reinterred in adjacent graves in Harlebeke New British Cemetery.

It seems rather vainglorious to identify your son by your own title or rank, as Sir George and Lady Whitehead have done, but Reginald Griffiths' parents have done the same:

> Son of Owen
> And Hetty Griffiths
> Aberavon, S. Wales
> Deus vult

And both parents have used Deus vult, God wills it. It suggests that they might have conferred, which is rather poignant since the Whiteheads and the Griffiths came from different worlds. It is enough to say that the seven members of the Whitehead family – and their seven servants – lived in Wilmington Hall, Dartford, Kent a house with six drawing rooms and eleven bedrooms, whilst the nine members of the Griffiths household lived in Aberavon, Glamorganshire in a six-roomed house that was also their shop – Owen Griffiths and Sons Fruiterer, Fish, Game and Poultry Dealer.

In March 1919, George Whitehead's younger brother, James, died of war related illness. Sir George died in 1931 leaving a bequest of £10,000 to the University of Oxford to be known as the James Hugh Edendale Whitehead and the George William Edendale Whitehead Memorial Fund for the promotion of the study of history and/or the literature of England and her colonies. The title passed to Sir George's younger brother.

LOVE NEVER FAILETH

THE REVEREND THEODORE BAYLEY HARDY VC, DSO, MC
ARMY CHAPLAINS DEPARTMENT
DIED 18 OCTOBER 1918 AGED 54
BURIED ST SEVER CEMETERY EXTENSION, ROUEN, FRANCE

There is a memorial plaque in Carlisle Cathedral that reads:

> In memory of Theodore Bayley Hardy Vicar of Hutton Roof. Appointed C.F.
> Aug. 1916: Attached 8th Lincs. Regt & 8th Somerset Lt Infantry. Awarded
> D.S.O. July 1917: M.C. Oct. 1917: Victoria Cross April 1918. Chaplain to the
> King Sept. 1918. Was Wounded Oct. 1918. Died at Rouen Oct. 18 1918.
> This tablet is erected as part of a Diocesan tribute to His heroic courage,
> sympathetic service and spiritual labours.

When he joined the army in 1916, Hardy asked the Revd Geoffrey Studdart Kennedy for advice on how best to get through to the soldiers. Studdart Kennedy told him:

> Live with the men, go everywhere they go ... share all their risks, and
> more ... The line is the key to the whole business. Work in the very
> front and they will listen to you ... Men will forgive you anything but
> lack of courage and devotion.

Two years later, after being awarded the Victoria Cross for 'conspicuous bravery and devotion to duty on many occasions', Hardy acknowledged that Studdart Kennedy's advice, 'more than any other in my life, has helped me in this work'.

After leading what must have seemed like a charmed existence, Hardy was wounded in the thigh by a machine gun bullet on 11 October 1918 during the crossing of the River Selle. He was taken to hospital where pneumonia set in and he died seven days later. His son, William Hastings Hardy, a doctor in the RAMC, chose his inscription. Hardy's wife had died in 1914. It comes from *1 Corinthians 13:8* The Revised Version

> Love suffereth long, and is kind; love envieth not; love vaunteth not itself,
> is not puffed up, doth not behave itself unseemly, seeketh not its own, is
> not provoked, taketh not account of evil; rejoiceth not in unrighteousness,
> but rejoiceth with the truth; beareth all things, believeth all things, hopeth
> all things, endureth all things. Love never faileth.

LOVE AND KISSES FROM MOTHER

PRIVATE JAMES DONNELLY
ROYAL DUBLIN FUSILIERS
DIED 19 OCTOBER 1918 AGED 19
BURIED ROISEL COMMUNAL CEMETERY EXTENSION, FRANCE

James Donnelly was nineteen when he died of wounds in a Casualty Clearing Station at Roisel on 19 October 1918. He was his mother's only child. Her first husband, James's father, died before his son was two. She had since remarried a man called William Patterson who owned a bar in Newbridge, Co. Kildare.

Donnelly's medal index card shows that he was entitled to the 1915 Star having served in a theatre of war, identified as '2b' – Gallipoli and the Aegean Islands – since 28 August 1915. At this date he can have been no more than sixteen since he was only eleven on the 2 April 1911, the day the Irish census was taken.

His Gallipoli service would either have been with the 1st or 6th Battalion Royal Dublin Fusiliers but by the autumn of 1918 Donnelly was serving with the 2nd Battalion. On the 16 October the battalion took over the front line at Saint Benin just south of Le Cateau. On the morning of the 17th they crossed the River Selle in the face of heavy machine gun fire and two attempted German counter-attacks. Relieved in the early hours of the 19th, during the preceding four days the battalion had suffered over two hundred casualties, among them over 160 wounded. Donnelly died of wounds that day.

Mrs Ann Patterson signed for her son's inscription, which is all the more moving for its simple informality.

NO THOUGHT OF GLORY
TO BE WON
THERE WAS HIS DUTY TO BE DONE
AND HE DID IT

PRIVATE JOHN O'NEILL
ROYAL WELSH FUSILIERS
DIED 20 OCTOBER 1918 AGED 20
BURIED GLAGEON COMMUNAL CEMETERY EXTENSION, FRANCE

This matter-of-fact statement is repeated five times in *Promoted*, the poem John Oxenham wrote in praise of sixteen-year-old John Travers Cornwell who, although mortally wounded, remained at his post on HMS *Chester* throughout the Battle of Jutland whilst the rest of his gun crew lay dead or dying around him.

> Wounded when scarce the fight begun,
> Of all his fellows left not one;
> There was his duty to be done, –
> And he did it.

John O'Neill came from Birkenhead where his father was a gas fitter at the shipyard. He served with 9th Battalion Royal Welsh Fusiliers and died on 20 October 1918, when the battalion attacked the high ground to the east of the River Selle. According to the battalion diary, 'All objectives were gained. Gains were consolidated and held'.

O'Neill is buried in Glageon, over 50 km east of where the Fusiliers attacked. The town had been occupied by the Germans since the beginning of the war and was not liberated until early November. It would appear that O'Neill was taken prisoner and died in German hands.

His father chose his inscription, attributing to his son that same sense of duty that Oxenham had attributed to Jack Cornwall:

> Britain, be proud of such a son! –
> Deathless the fame that he has won.
> Only a boy, – but such a one! –
> Standing for ever to his gun;
> There was his duty to be done, –
> And he did it.

HIS MEN USED TO SAY "WE WOULD FOLLOW 'TOMMY' ANYWHERE"

CAPTAIN HOWARD VICTOR FRASER THOMAS MC
ROYAL SCOTS
DIED 22 OCTOBER 1918 AGED 21
BURIED HARLEBEKE NEW BRITISH CEMETERY, BELGIUM

Howard Thomas left Winchester in the summer of 1915, just after his eighteenth birthday. Commissioned into the Royal Scots that September, he went with them to France the following May, just before his nineteenth birthday. Two years later, at the age of twenty-one, he was a captain with a Military Cross, which he won for his actions during the Battle of Arras in April 1917. The citation reads:

> He led his platoon to the second objective with great courage, where he organised a party and outflanked the enemy, enfilading them, inflicting heavy losses. He was wounded but carried on throughout the day.

Thomas did not return to France until May 1918. Five months later, on 22 October, he led his company in the 9th Division's capture of the village of Vichte and was killed outright by a machine gun bullet in his head.

His father, Henry Dewdney Thomas, the headmaster of Cargilfield, a prep school in Edinburgh, chose his inscription, quoting from a letter of condolence written by a senior officer. For it to be said that your men would follow you anywhere was a great tribute; *A General's Letters to His Son on Obtaining His Commission* (1917) makes the point:

> In a well disciplined unit men find it almost impossible not to obey the commander's voice, however terrible the order.

But:

> ... it is as important to look after your men, and keep them fit, as it is to lead them well in action. If you look after your men, and if they know that in you they have a friend upon whom they may depend, you may rely on their never leaving you in the lurch.

It would appear that Captain 'Tommy' Thomas MC had acquired the knack of combining discipline with friendship.

"HE WAS A VERY FINE FELLOW AND BRAVE, FOR HE KEPT ON WITH HIS LEWIS GUN ALL THE WAY DOWN" THE PILOT

SECOND LIEUTENANT FREDERICK HORACE REED
ROYAL AIR FORCE
DIED BETWEEN 23 & 27 OCTOBER 1918 AGED 20
BURIED TERLINCTHUN BRITISH CEMETERY, WIMILLE, FRANCE

Frederick Horace Reed served as an observer with 6 Squadron RAF. He and his pilot were reported missing on 23 October 1918. His father received no further news until late 1919 when the pilot, who had been taken prisoner, reported that although their plane had been surrounded, Reed's skilful use of his machine gun had enabled him to bring it down safely – behind the German lines. It is the pilot's words that are on Reed's headstone: 'Until I stepped out of the machine, I never knew Horace was wounded. He was a very fine fellow and brave, for he kept on with his Lewis gun all the way down'.

Walter Reed, Horace Reed's father, now knew his son had been wounded and taken prisoner but nothing else. Then in September 1920 the body of an 'unknown British aviator' was exhumed from Englefontaine Churchyard. The exhumation form, which shows that there was nothing in the grave to identify the man, is stamped: 'Dame Adelaide Livingstone Informed'. Dame Adelaide was a remarkable American woman who, at the end of the war:

> was appointed the Army Council head of the War Office mission to trace British soldiers reported as 'missing' in France and Flanders. In this capacity she travelled widely in Europe ... Between 1920 and April 1922 she was assistant director of Graves Registration and Enquiries in central Europe ... For her wartime services she was among the first women to be created DBE in 1918.
> *Oxford Dictionary of National Biography*

By 1930 Reed's body had been identified. In 1975, his grave, together with the only other three Commonwealth graves in the cemetery, were moved to Terlincthun Military Cemetery as part of the Commission's policy of removing graves from isolated sites where it is difficult to assure maintenance.

TERLINCTHUN BRITISH
CEMETERY

SO HE PASSED OVER
AND ALL THE TRUMPETS SOUNDED
FOR HIM ON THE OTHER SIDE

PRIVATE ERNEST DAVISON

CHESHIRE REGIMENT

DIED 23 OCTOBER 1918 AGED 23

BURIED AMERVAL COMMUNAL CEMETERY EXTENSION, SOLESMES, FRANCE

Ernest Davison's inscription describes the death of Mr Valiant-for-Truth, a good man in John Bunyan's *Pilgrim's Progress*. The trumpets sound for him as he crosses the river of death to the Celestial City, the New Jerusalem.

> When the day that he must go hence was come, many accompanied
> him to the Riverside, into which as he went he said, Death where is
> thy sting? And as he went down deeper he said, Grave, where is thy
> victory? So he passed over, and all the Trumpets sounded for him on
> the other side.

And why did the trumpets sound? Because it is a sign that the dead man was one of God's chosen. In the minds of many people affected by the Great War, the words of *St Matthew 24:31* resonated with special force:

> 'there will be a time of great tribulation, nation will rise up against
> nation, and kingdom against kingdom after which Christ will 'send his
> angels with a great sound of a trumpet, and they shall gather together
> his elect from the four winds, ... '.

To Mr John Davison, Private Davison's father, the trumpets sounded at the death of his son to signify that he too was worthy of reaching the Celestial City because he had died in the service of Christ – fighting the Germans.

Davison served with the 1st Battalion Cheshire Regiment and was killed in action on the 23 October during the Battle of the Selle. He was originally buried in Contour British Cemetery in a single grave with a sergeant and three other privates; the bodies were exhumed and reburied separately in Amerval Communal British Cemetery in 1923.

PRO DEO ET PATRIA
"MOTHER DEAR I MUST GO"

GUNNER ARNOLD ALEXANDER MACULLY
AUSTRALIAN FIELD ARTILLERY
DIED 23 OCTOBER 1918 AGED 24
BURIED PRÉMONT BRITISH CEMETERY, FRANCE

Arnold Macully was a volunteer. Every Australian soldier was a volunteer since there was no conscription in the country. But it was a bitterly divisive issue over which the Government held a referendum in October 1916. The country voted against conscription by a margin of 72,000. It held a second referendum in December 1917 but this time lost by 166,588 votes.

This is what lies behind Mrs Macully's choice of inscription. Her son, Arnold, had decided that he had a duty to fight for God and his country – the Latin 'Deo et patria' lending gravitas to the sentiment. But she had not forced him to do his duty: 'Mother dear I must go' speaks of a tender but determined son and a mother who is unwilling to part with him. The implication is clear, Arnold Macully was no shirker and Mrs Macully had not forced her son to enlist.

Macully served with the 14th Brigade Australian Artillery. All Australian divisions had been withdrawn from the Western Front after the Battle of Montbrehain on the 5 October. Having been in continuous action since August, they were exhausted. Due to casualties, some battalions were operating at less than half their strength and were close to breaking point; the problem was exacerbated by the lack of volunteers and reinforcements. However, some artillery units remained in support of the British and American infantry. The 14th Brigade was one of those that remained. On 22 October they were engaged at Le Cateau, providing a creeping barrage for a British attack. Macully was one of twelve other ranks injured by shellfire. A witness told the Red Cross:

> It happened at dusk one evening late in October, and Gunner Macully was in his dugout in the waggon lines when he was badly wounded by a shell in the thigh and side. His mate helped place him on a stretcher, and carried him to an Ambulance by the road-side. He was quite conscious and chatted cheerfully to the Drivers Saunders and Edwards, telling them how to apply the Field Dressing. He was then taken away, and they learnt later that he had succumbed to his wounds.

HE LIKE A SOLDIER FELL

PRIVATE GEORGE HORNER
CAMERONIANS (SCOTTISH RIFLES)
DIED 24 OCTOBER 1918 AGED 21
BURIED HIGHLAND CEMETERY, LE CATEAU, FRANCE

Oh let me like a soldier fall
Upon some open plain –
This breast expanding for a ball
To blot out every stain.
Brave manly hearts confer my doom,
That gentler ones may tell;
Howe'er unknown forgot my tomb
He, like a soldier fell.
He, like a soldier fell.

This is a song from the ballad opera *Maritana*, written in 1845 by William Vincent Wallace and Edward Fitzball. There is no soldier in the opera, just a roguish hero, Don Caesar, who is to be hanged for duelling. At the last moment he is offered a choice between a soldier's death – by firing squad – or public hanging. He chooses the firing squad so that it can be said of him that 'he like a soldier fell'.

George Horner's father chose his inscription, probably completely unaware of its context since the song, long since detached from the opera, regularly featured in popular collections of patriotic songs.

Born and brought up in Kilmarnock, George Horner was the son of John Horner, a forge labourer, and his wife Jeanie. He served with the 1st Battalion Cameronians (Scottish Rifles) and was killed on 24 October 1918 in the attack on Engelfontaine, either during the action on the 24th or that night when the Germans shelled the British lines with a large proportion of gas shells. Engelfontaine fell the next day. Horner was among those missing after the action; his body found after the war at an isolated burial site; it was exhumed and reburied in Highland Cemetery.

ENLISTED AUGUST 1914
LIVE THOU FOR ENGLAND
I FOR ENGLAND DIED

CORPORAL RICHARD WHITAKER LEITH PEMELL
ROYAL FUSILIERS
DIED 25 OCTOBER 1918 AGED 36
BURIED HEESTERT MILITARY CEMETERY, BELGIUM

Richard Pemell, a stock brokers' clerk in the City of London, joined the 17th Battalion Royal Fusiliers on 31 August 1914, the day it was formed. In November 1915, two months after his marriage to Annie Mary Stone, the battalion landed in France. By the time of his death Pemell was a corporal in 'A' Company, 26th Battalion. On 25 October 1918 the battalion attacked towards the River Scheldt but was held up near Ooteghem by an intense German barrage and machine gun fire. 'A' Company attempted to:

> rush the windmill on the ridge south-west of Ooteghem. Lieutenant T
> Robinson, of A Company was killed in a first gallant dash; but it was
> eventually captured. After further heavy losses ... the battalion dug in
> for the night. Fighting patrols were pushed forward next day, but the
> battalion were relieved before they reached the Scheldt, and the battle
> line saw them no more.
> *The Royal Fusiliers in the Great War* H.C. O'Neill 1922 p 327

Pemell, who had joined the 17th Battalion Royal Fusiliers on the day it was formed, transferred to the 26th Battalion and was killed the day before its last engagement.

Mrs Annie Pemell drew attention to the poignancy of her husband's dates of service in the first line of his inscription. The next lines are adapted from an epitaph that had appeared in *The Times* on 16 February 1918 under the heading, For a Memorial Tablet:

> True love by life – true love by death – is tried:
> Live thou for England! – we for England died.
> February, 1918.   A.C.A.

A.C.A. is thought to have been Arthur Campbell Ainger (1841–1919), who taught Classics at Eton for nearly forty years and was the author of a number of hymns including, *God Moves in a Mysterious Way.*

DARLING BOY
GOD MUST BE RIGHT
MUM AND DAD

PRIVATE CHARLES B PARKER
CAMERON HIGHLANDERS
DIED 25 OCTOBER 1918 AGED 34
BURIED HIGHLAND CEMETERY, LE CATEAU, FRANCE

Many families made their acceptance of God's will evident by such inscriptions as, 'Thy will be done', 'We cannot Lord Thy purpose see but all is well that's done by thee', 'Not my will but Thine O Lord'. Private Parker's inscription is different: there's an air of disbelief to it, as if his mother is struggling to believe that it can have been 'right' for God to take her 'darling boy', her only surviving child. And yet he had.

Charles Parker's parents were in the theatre. Haidee Parker, his mother, described herself as 'Dancer ex' in the 1891 census, Frank Parker, his father, as a Stage Manager. By 1901 Frank Parker was the theatrical manager of the London Hippodrome and in 1911 he described himself as a 'producer of plays'. In 1911 his son, Charles Parker, described himself as a 'Box Office Keeper'.

Parker served with the 1st Battalion Queen's Own Cameron Highlanders and was killed in action on 25 October 1918, the last day of the Battle of the Selle. The war was nearly over: Cambrai had fallen on 8 October, the Germans had abandoned the Hindenburg Line, the Selle had been crossed and the armies were fighting now in open country. Parker's body was recovered from an isolated grave in March 1920.

ALL OUR BEAUTY
AND HOPE AND JOY
WE OWE TO LADS LIKE YOU

PRIVATE ROBERT T INGLIS
CHESHIRE REGIMENT
DIED 28 OCTOBER 1918 AGED 19
BURIED NIEDERZWEHREN CEMETERY, KASSEL, GERMANY

Robert Inglis, who served with the 10th Battalion Cheshire Regiment, not the 19th as it says on his War Grave Commission record, was taken prisoner, unwounded, when the Germans overran the catacombs at Hill 63 near Ploegsteert Wood on 11 April 1918. Held at Friedrichsfeld bei Wesel prisoner of war camp, he died six months later, the cause unrecorded.

Robert's father, Alexander Inglis, a stableman from Newlands near Glasgow, chose his inscription. It comes from the last lines of *Young Fellow My Lad* by the English-born, Canadian poet Robert Service. In the poem, a father tries to tell his son that he is too young to join up, to which the son replies: 'I'm seventeen and a quarter, Dad, and ever so strong you know'. The son goes off to fight and the father hears nothing from him. He's very afraid:

> I hear them tell that we've gained new ground,
> But a terrible price we've paid:
> God grant, my boy, that you're safe and sound;
> But oh I'm afraid, afraid.

Eventually he gets news: 'They've told me the truth, young fellow my lad: You'll never come back again'. But the father's comfort is the thought that his son lives on:

> In the gleam of the evening star,
> In the wood-note wild and the laugh of the child,
> In all sweet things that are.
> And you'll never die, my wonderful boy,
> While life is noble and true;
> For all our beauty and hope and joy
> We will owe to lads like you.

"WE ALL LOVED HIM AS A BRAVE SOLDIER AND A STRAIGHT WHITE MAN" EXTRACT OFFICER'S LETTER

PRIVATE THOMAS HARRY MANN
EAST KENT REGIMENT (THE BUFFS)
DIED 31 OCTOBER 1918 AGED 19
BURIED MONTAY BRITISH CEMETERY, FRANCE

What a difference a hundred years makes: our understanding of the words 'straight' and 'white', especially in relation to men, has changed radically since Private Mann's officer described him as 'a straight white man'. To be straight meant to be honest and straightforward, and to be a white man meant to be decent and trustworthy.

On the 2 October 1915, Thomas Harry Mann enlisted in the King's Royal Rifle Corps. He said he was nineteen. Four months later he was serving in France. But three months after this, on 3 May 1916, he was discharged from the army. Why? According to the record, he was 'Discharged having made misstatement as to age on enlistment'. Thomas Mann wasn't nineteen when he enlisted he was only sixteen. Nevertheless, despite the 'misstatement', someone has written on his discharge form:

> A good brave lad who has been four months at the front and he is willing and hard working.

Did his parents track him down and tell the authorities how old he was or did Thomas himself ask to be released when faced with the reality of war? The records don't say.

Mann enlisted again in September 1917, this time in the 7th Battalion The Buffs (East Kent Regiment). He was killed in action on 31 October 1918 when all the 7th Battalion's war diary has to say of the day is:

> During night our patrols active and a number of enemy machine guns located. A patrol under 2/Lt Gerard endeavoured to capture an enemy MG post but came under heavy fire. Bombs were thrown and the gun was afterwards inactive.

"I WAS EVER A FIGHTER. SO ONE FIGHT MORE THE BEST AND THE LAST"

LIEUTENANT ARTHUR ROWLAND SKEMP
GLOUCESTERSHIRE REGIMENT
DIED 1 NOVEMBER 1918 AGED 36
BURIED HIGHLAND CEMETERY, LE CATEAU, FRANCE

Jessie Skemp chose her husband's inscription from Robert Browning's, *Prospice*; an appropriate choice for Lieutenant Skemp who was the Winterstoke Professor of English at the University of Bristol and a Browning authority. In the poem, Browning expresses a determination not to hide from death but to meet it head on:

> I was ever a fighter, so – one fight more,
> The best and the last!
> I would hate that death bandaged my eyes, and forebore,
> And bade me creep past.
> No! let me taste the whole of it, fare like my peers,
> The heroes of old,
> Bear the brunt, in a minute pay glad life's arrears
> Of pain, darkness and cold.

Skemp had both studied and taught in Germany, where he had many friends; nevertheless he enlisted straightaway and was given a role in the University of Bristol Officer Training Corps. Here his teaching skills were effectively transferred to the training of officers. In the summer of 1918 he got his wish, a commission in the 1st Battalion Gloucestershire Regiment. Posted to France, he arrived at the end of October. On the 30th the battalion took over the line NE of Mazinghien, on the 31st it repulsed an enemy attack; the next day the enemy attacked again and although they were repulsed, Skemp and six soldiers were killed. He had been at the front scarcely eight days.

The University, his family and friends were devastated, as a colleague wrote in a widely published appreciation:

> His remarkable powers as a lecturer on his subject were well known, and he was idolised by staff and students alike for his intellectual gifts, strong and virile character, his energy and enthusiasm, and his geniality and unfailing kindness of heart endeared him to all.

ENLISTED AUG. 23 1914
"HE SLEEPS
WITH ENGLAND'S HEROES
IN THE WATCHFUL CARE OF GOD"

SECOND LIEUTENANT ERNEST CARTWRIGHT
DUKE OF WELLINGTON'S WEST RIDING REGIMENT
DIED 1 NOVEMBER 1918 AGED 26
BURIED MAING COMMUNAL CEMETERY EXTENSION, FRANCE

The date in Cartwright's inscription not only highlights the fact that he was a volunteer, but that he was a very early volunteer. He joined the West Riding Regiment in the first month of the war and went with it to France on 15 July 1915. Three years later, Cartwright, who had enlisted as a private, was commissioned into his old regiment as a second lieutenant in the 6th Battalion, serving in B Company.

During the night of 31 October/1 November 1918 the war diary recorded that the companies formed up to force a crossing across the River Rhonelle. B Company was in front.

> Zero was 05.15. The Barrage was splendidly intense and accurate. The
> Bridges were carried and put into good positions – a very large number
> of machine gun posts were overcome, many Boche killed and hundreds
> of prisoners.

One would hope this meant that 'hundreds of prisoners' were taken rather than that 'hundreds of prisoners' were killed. Second Lieutenant Cartwright was among the dead. The second part of Cartwright's inscription comes from an anonymous poem first published in 1916 in a newspaper *In Memoriam* column. The last two lines of the second verse became a very popular inscription.

> Gone without one farewell message.
> Mangled by a German shell,
> He, whose laughter still is ringing
> In the home he loved so well.
>
> Comrade's hands, by love made tender,
> Laid our warrior 'neath the sod,
> And he sleeps with England's heroes
> In the watchful care of God.

O WIND
IF WINTER COMES
CAN SPRING BE FAR BEHIND?

CAPTAIN HARRY DUNLOP, MC
CANADIAN ARMY MEDICAL CORPS
DIED 2 NOVEMBER 1918 AGED 34
BURIED AULNOY COMMUNAL CEMETERY, FRANCE

War Diary
102nd Battalion Canadian Infantry
Aulnoy
Saturday November 2 1918
The Hun started bombing and shelling at 04:00 hours. Our barrage opened at 05:30 hours ... The Hun continued desultory shelling of the town and at about 09:00 hours, the Battalion Medical Officer, Captain Harry Dunlop MC (CAMC) was hit in the head whilst standing in the doorway of HQ and died shortly afterwards, to the intense sorrow of all.

Dunlop was working in Peru when the war broke out. He returned to Canada, enlisted in March 1916 and went to Europe in October. In March 1918 he married Rachel Thayer, an American, in London. In August 1918 he was awarded a Military Cross for:

Conspicuous gallantry and devotion to duty; this officer followed close behind the attack, and attended to the wounded under heavy machine gun fire. He was untiring in his efforts to care for and evacuate the wounded, and undoubtedly saved many lives.

Mrs Dunlop, who returned to the United States after the war, chose her husband's inscription from the last line of Shelley's *Ode to the West Wind*. The poem, written in 1819, expresses Shelley's support for the people of Europe in their struggle against authoritarian regimes. Winter in this context meant the suppression of liberal protest and the re-establishment of reactionary governments after the signing of the Treaty of Vienna in 1815. To Shelley, just as spring always follows winter, so conservative repression will always be followed by liberal reforms. And in the context of Harry Dunlop's inscription, there is the suggestion that death will also be followed by new life.

FORTH FROM THE CONFLICT UNASHAMED HE PASSED VICTORIOUS ON HIS WAY

CAPTAIN THOMAS CHARLES RICHMOND BAKER, DFC, MM & BAR
AUSTRALIAN FLYING CORPS
DIED 4 NOVEMBER 1918
BURIED ESCANAFFLES COMMUNAL CEMETERY, HAINAULT, BELGIUM

After spending two years in the Australian Field Artillery, Thomas Baker joined the Australian Flying Corps in June 1918. At the time of his death four months later he had twelve confirmed 'victories' to his name. It took six to make you an ace. On 4 November his plane was attacked and brought down by Airshipdriver Lieut. von Hantelman whilst on a bombing raid behind the German lines. Hantelman contacted the British for confirmation of his twenty-sixth victory. He claimed that at 11.35 he had shot down 'a single-seated flying machine', which was 'smashed to pieces'.

Baker was assumed to be dead. In September 1920 the body of an unknown 'British Flying Officer' was exhumed and later reburied in Escanaffles Communal Cemetery. According to the exhumation report the clothing had rotted away, there was no identity disc and the body was too broken and decayed for it to be possible to identify either hair colour or height. The bottom of the report had a pencil note: 'Copy to Dame Livingstone', the American head of the War Office mission to trace British soldiers reported as missing in France and Flanders.

Baker's body had still not been identified by 1927 when his mother filled in the circular for the Roll of Honour of Australia. Beside the question, 'Place where killed or wounded?' Mrs Baker wrote, 'France or Belgium no record'. Yet today the grave in Escanaffles Communal Cemetery carries his name. His mother chose his inscription. It comes from verse six of *The Good End* by Harold Begbie, published in the *Daily Mail* in October 1905 to mark the centenary of the death of Admiral Lord Nelson at the Battle of Trafalgar:

> Dishonour tarnished not his flag, no stain upon his battles lay,
> Forth from the conflict, unashamed, he passed victorious on his way;
> Forth from the conflict, unashamed, with thanks to God, without a sigh.
> So died for England's sake, this man, and whispered it was sweet to die.
> Draw near and mark with reverent mind
> How die the captains of mankind.

IS THIS THE END?

PRIVATE CHARLES JAMES BOLTON
ROYAL ARMY MEDICAL CORPS
DIED 4 NOVEMBER 1918 AGED 37
BURIED LA VALLÉE-MULÂTRE COMMUNAL CEMETERY EXTENSION, FRANCE

This is an unusual headstone inscription. Most families were far more likely to assert a belief in the afterlife than to question it. For some it was a matter of firm Christian belief: 'In sure and certain hope of the resurrection'. For others it was more of a secular hope: 'Only goodnight beloved, not farewell'; 'We shall meet again from all at home'. And then there were the Spiritualists: 'Yet he is here with us today a thousand things his touch reveals'; 'Though absent in the body he still talks with us'. But Private Bolton's wife, Eva, was not so sure – 'Is this the end?'

Private Bolton, a house painter from Norwich, served as a stretcher bearer with the 2nd Field Ambulance. He was shot by a sniper whilst bringing in the wounded during the 1st Division's attack on the Sambre-Oise Canal.

Was it against the Geneva Convention to shoot a stretcher bearer, should he not have been protected by the Red Cross brassard, an arm band with a red cross on it, that he would have been wearing? The 1906 Convention decreed that:

> the sick and wounded must be taken care of irrespective of nationality;
> that medical personnel must, as far as military exigencies permit, be
> left in charge of sick and wounded, and that, when they are captured
> by the enemy, they are to continue their duty under his directions ...

The same kind of protection was to be given to personnel in charge of convoys of wounded and those carrying weapons to guard the sick and wounded, none of whom were to be regarded as prisoners of war if they fell into enemy hands. But,

> As regimental stretcher bearers are not exclusively engaged in the care
> of the wounded they are not entitled, as such, to protection under the
> Convention or to wear the Red Cross Brassard.

Regimental stretcher bearers, those who sometimes bore arms and sometimes carried stretchers, wore arm bands with the letters SB on them. But Bolton, as a member of the RAMC, would have worn one with a red cross on it. In theory this should have protected him from being the object of a sniper's aim – but it did not.

"SHALL LIFE RENEW THESE BODIES? OF A TRUTH ALL DEATH WILL HE ANNUL" W.O.

LIEUTENANT WILFRED EDWARD OWEN, MC
MANCHESTER REGIMENT
DIED 4 NOVEMBER 1918 AGED 25
BURIED ORS COMMUNAL CEMETERY, FRANCE

A hundred years after his death Wilfred Owen is one of the most famous casualties of the war, and one of the best known of all the anti-war poets. In the summer of 1918, after being hospitalized in Britain with shell shock, Owen was given the opportunity of a home posting. But he decided he must return to the front:

> For leaning out last midnight on my sill,
> I heard the sighs of men that have no skill
> To speak of their distress, no, nor the will!
> A voice I know. And this time I must go.
> *The Calls*

Owen did not return just to give voice to the voiceless soldiery but to fight. He won a Military Cross for his actions on 1st/2nd October 1918 when he personally manipulated a captured enemy machine gun and inflicted 'considerable losses on the enemy'. He was killed a month later as he urged his men across the Sambre-Oise canal in the face the German machine guns.

Wilfred was the eldest child of Tom and Susan Owen who chose a line from *The End*, one of Wilfred's own poems, for his inscription. But, by shortening the line and omitting a question mark they gave it an opposite meaning to the one their son intended. The poem is a comment on the idea of resurrection, the Day of Judgement, Owen asks:

> Shall Life renew these bodies? Of a truth
> All death will he annul, all tears assuage?

There are two questions here. The inscription, as written by his parents, has only one and an answer: yes, God will annul all death at the Resurrection.

I LIE HERE MOTHER
BUT THE VICTORY IS OURS

LANCE CORPORAL ALEXANDER MACK MM
NORTHAMPTONSHIRE REGIMENT
DIED 5 NOVEMBER 1918 AGED 32
BURIED BUSIGNY COMMUNAL CEMETERY EXTENSION, FRANCE

Alexander Mack died of wounds in a Casualty Clearing Station six days before the end of the war; could he have known that victory was in sight? The Germans were still putting up a fierce resistance but the Allies were daily pushing them further and further back towards Germany. Turkey had already surrendered on 30 October, as had Austria on 3 November and two days after Mack's death, General Hindenburg, the head of the German Army, opened peace negotiations with the Allies.

Mack might have known that military victory was in sight, but is this what his mother meant by the words she chose? When Christians talk of victory they mean Christ's victory over death, as summarised in *1 Corinthians 15: 54-56*

> Death is swallowed up in victory. O death, where is thy sting? O grave, where is thy victory? The sting of death is sin; and the strength of sin is the law. But thanks be to God, which giveth us the victory through our Lord Jesus Christ.

The passage was the inspiration for a hymn by the Scottish-born Presbyterian minister William H. Drummond (1772–1865), of which this is the first verse:

> Thanks be to God, the Lord,
> The victory is ours;
> And hell is overcome
> By Christ's triumphant pow'rs!
> The monster sin in chains is bound,
> And death has felt his mortal wound.

Was Mrs Mary Mack conflating Christ's victory over death with the British victory over the Germans, and did she see 'the monster' as Germany?

Born in Scotland but brought up in London, Alexander Mack was a printer's machine minder, responsible for the flow of the ink and the pressure of the roller as the pages were printed. He served with the 6th Battalion Northamptonshire Regiment and died of wounds sustained in the fighting for the Sambre-Oise Canal.

KISMET

SECOND LIEUTENANT ARCHIBALD HUNTER
KING'S OWN YORKSHIRE LIGHT INFANTRY
DIED 7 NOVEMBER 1918 AGED 19
BURIED DOURLERS COMMUNAL CEMETERY EXTENSION, FRANCE

The word kismet derives from the Turkish word *qismet* or the Arabic *qismat*. In these cultures it means the will of Allah. The word appears several times as an inscription among the casualties of the last few weeks of the war, and it is the inscription on the grave of a soldier – a veteran of the South African War and of the North West Frontier – who was killed in action on 23 August 1914, the first day the British Army engaged with the enemy on the Western Front.

Archibald Hunter, a fifteen-year-old schoolboy in Durham when the war broke out, was commissioned into the King's Own Yorkshire Light Infantry on 30 July 1918, just after his nineteenth birthday. He served with the 9th Battalion, which was initially in reserve when the 70th Brigade launched an unsuccessful attack towards the Avesne Maubeuge road on 7 November. The 9th Battalion war diary relates what happened when they were ordered to lead another attack at 16.50:

> From now onwards this Battalion, ably led, made excellent progress, and literally carried everything before it by sheer determination and will to win. A strong stand was made by the enemy, but all to no purpose. In the fierce fighting that took place in front and in the streets of the villages, men of the 9th K.O.Yorks. L.I. refused to be denied the victory, which they had set out to gain. Once again the enemy were entirely outmanoeuvred and outfought. By 21.30 hrs. so great had been the force of the assault, the villages of Limont Fontaine and Eclaibes – thoroughly cleared of the enemy, were added to the growing list of Allied gains.

The war had four days to run and Hunter, who had been at the front for only three months was dead.

In 1911, the play *Kismet*, by Edward Knoblock, appeared on the London stage where it ran for two years, being made into a film in 1914. It was only a very slight love story but it elevated the word in the public's consciousness, not as 'the will of Allah', and definitely not as the will of God, but as random chance.

INSTEAD OF LAMENTATION
THEY HAVE REMEMBRANCE

LIEUTENANT WILLIAM HAROLD WILLIAMS
ROYAL GARRISON ARTILLERY
DIED 9 NOVEMBER 1918
BURIED JEMAPPES COMMUNAL CEMETERY, BELGIUM

There are nine identified British soldiers buried in Jemappes Communal Cemetery, one from the second day of British fighting on the Western Front, one from the second month, and seven from the last three days of the war. Jemappes is a few miles west of Mons – the British Army was back where it had been in August 1914.

There is very little to identify Williams: we have his Christian names and his date of death, we know that he served with the 326th Siege Battery and that a Mrs Williams, 8 Repton Avenue, Gidea Park, Romford, Kent, chose his inscription but whether she was his wife or his mother we cannot tell. Without knowing his age and the Christian name of a parent it is difficult to get any further.

Williams' inscription is a translation of a lyric fragment by Simonides honouring the Greeks who died at the Battle of Thermopylae in 480 BC.

> Of those who died at Thermopylae their fortune is glorious, and their fate lovely; their tomb is an altar, in place of lamentation there is remembrance, and pity becomes praise.

The fragment is better known in the translation by Arthur Burrell, which was published in *At the Front: A Pocket Book of Verse* (1915), a collection of patriotic poems by authors ranging from William Shakespeare to Rupert Brooke.

Mrs Williams used Burrell's translation.

> Of them that died in Thermopylae
> Glorious was the fortune: fair is the fate.
> For a tomb they have an altar,
> For lamentation, memory,
> And for pity, praise.

I.H.S.
ONE OF ENGLAND'S
GLORIOUS DEAD

PRIVATE ALBERT BETHEL
ARMY SERVICE CORPS
DIED 10 NOVEMBER 1918 AGED 27
BURIED ST SEVER CEMETERY EXTENSION, ROUEN, FRANCE

'The Glorious Dead', are the only three words on the Cenotaph in Whitehall, the British Empire's memorial to its dead of two world wars. Designed in 1919 by Sir Edward Lutyens (1869-1944), the cenotaph is admired for its austere appropriateness – a cenotaph is an empty tomb symbolising the absent dead – but some see the inscription as 'problematic'. Why? Because there is absolutely nothing glorious about dying in war. The word glorious is meant, however, to apply to the dead not to the manner of their dying. The dead have acquired glory by dying for their country. They have become glorious.

With its Christian, classical and military associations, it is a clever choice of word. To the Christian, glory is associated with God; it is His magnificence, His majesty, in which the righteous all share at their own deaths. In the Classical world, glory is renown, a good name acquired by noble actions. In Homer's *Iliad*, glory, *kleos*, is acquired on the battlefield, fighting bravely, risking death, dying. It is an intangible quality, something that only exists in the minds of others. It cannot be bought or awarded it can only be earned. And once a good name has been earned, it bestows a form of immortality – 'Their name liveth for evermore'.

Some claim Rudyard Kipling chose the words, others that it was Lloyd George, but according to a document in the National Archives, it was Lutyens himself. In 1930 he wrote: "'The glorious dead', the words I put on my original sketch, also survived unchanged". The words were part of his desire that the Cenotaph should express a simple reverence for those of all creeds and denominations who had fought and died in the war. But he had not composed a new term, Dryden, Pope, Shelley and Wordsworth all used 'the glorious dead' to describe the illustrious dead of their own eras.

Albert Bethel's wife, Isabella, chose his inscription. Born and brought up in Atherton, Lancashire, Bethel was a cotton spinner, married and with two children, when he joined the army in 1917. He served in the Mechanical Transport Company of the Army Service Corps and died of wounds in hospital in Rouen.

The initials I.H.S. in the first line of the inscription form a sacred monogram based on the first three letters of the name Jesus in Greek.

St Sever Cemetery

TO MY DEAR SON, ONE OF THREE
WHO GAVE THEIR LIVES
FOR THE COUNTRY

PRIVATE LEONARD CLIFTON BROCK
WILTSHIRE REGIMENT
DIED 11 NOVEMBER 1918 AGED 24
BURIED COLOGNE SOUTHERN CEMETERY, GERMANY

Francis and Hannah Brock had ten children, six sons and four daughters. The eldest three sons, Francis, Leonard and William all died during the First World War.

Lance Corporal Francis Edward Brock, 6th Wiltshire Regiment, died of wounds in a Casualty Clearing Station in Contay on 16 November 1916. He was twenty-four. His wife, Elizabeth, chose his inscription:

> Ever in our thoughts
> From your loving wife
> And daughter Lizzie

Four months later, Rifleman William John Brock, 1st/6th Battalion London Regiment, died of wounds in a Casualty Clearing Station in Lijssenthoek, Belgium. He was twenty. His mother chose his inscription:

> Be thou faithful unto death
> And I will give thee
> A crown of life

Private Leonard Clifton Brock, 1st Battalion Wiltshire Regiment, died as a German prisoner-of-war on 11 November 1918. He was twenty-four. His father chose his inscription remembering all three of his 'dear sons' who gave their lives for 'the country', note the lack of possessive pronoun.

In March 1965 a Mrs A.V. Alford wrote to the War Graves Commission to ask for confirmation of the burial particulars of three brothers, Francis, Leonard and William Brock, as she was going to be taking a holiday in France and Germany. The reply, signed by the Director General, told here where the three brothers were buried and added the extra information that they were the sons of Mr and Mrs Francis Brock of Hackney, London. Mrs A.V. Alford would have known that. She was born Annie Violet Brock, she was their sister; after nearly fifty years she was going to visit her brothers.

AD FINEM FIDELIS

CAPTAIN DUNCAN RONALD GORDON MACKAY DFC
ROYAL AIR FORCE
DIED 11 NOVEMBER 1918 AGED 23
BURIED JOEUF COMMUNAL CEMETERY, FRANCE

Duncan Mackay left school in July 1914 and enlisted as a private in the Public Schools Battalion on 14 September, six weeks after the beginning of the war. He died of wounds on the day it ended, *Ad finem fidelis* – faithful to the end.

Mackay went to France with the 19th Battalion Royal Fusiliers on 14 November 1915, serving with them until June 1916 when he took a commission in the 13th Battalion Argyll and Sutherland Highlanders. He later transferred to the Royal Flying Corps as a pilot and served in France with 55 Squadron, a daylight bombing squadron. On 10 November 1918, he and his observer, Lieutenant H.T.C. Gompertz, were shot down returning from a raid. Both were taken prisoner. Mackay died the next day in hospital in the German city of Metz – German since 1871 when it was annexed from France at the end of the Franco-Prussian War. Returned to France at the end of the First World War, it was re-annexed by Germany following the fall of France in May 1940. It returned to France after 1945.

In December 1918, Mackay was awarded a posthumous DFC. The citation reads:

> An officer of conspicuous ability and determination, who, during the last four months of the fighting, has taken part in twenty-two bombing raids and three photographic reconnaissances, acting as leader on seven occasions. On 15 October he volunteered to carry out alone a bombing attack on an enemy aerodrome; low clouds and mist compelled him to fly at low altitudes varying from 800 to 1,000 feet. Having successfully reached his objective, he obtained two direct hits from a height of forty feet and stampeded horses with machine-gun fire. The cool courage and marked initiative shown by Captain Mackay in this operation merits high praise.

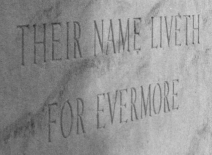

Tyne Cot Cemetery

EPITAPHS FEATURED IN THIS BOOK
BY CWGC CEMETERY

WARLENCOURT
BRITISH CEMETERY

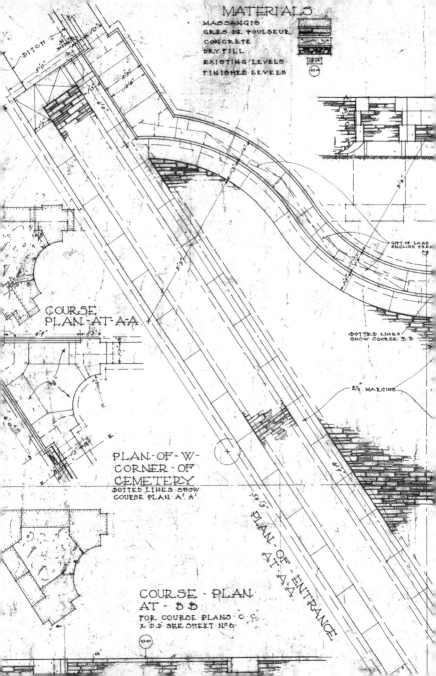

MATERIALS

MASSANGIS
GRES DE TOULSEUX
CONCRETE
DRY FILL
EXISTING LEVELS
FINISHED LEVELS

COURSE
PLAN · AT · A·A

PLAN · OF · W·
CORNER · OF·
CEMETERY
DOTTED LINES SHOW
COURSE PLAN A¹ A¹

COURSE · PLAN
AT · DD
FOR COURSE PLANS C C
& DD SEE SHEET N°6

GIFT OF LAND
ENGLISH FREN

DOTTED LINES
SHOW COURSE B B

2½" MARGINS

PLAN · OF · ENTRANCE
AT · A·A